GE
Your Sign, Your Day, Your Decan

Lisa Lazuli

Disclaimer

Copyright © May 2015 **GEMINI: Your Sign, Your Day, Your Decan** by Lisa Lazuli

All rights reserved. No part of this publication may be reproduced, distributed, or transmitted in any form or by any means, including photocopying, recording, or other electronic or mechanical methods, without the prior written permission of the publisher, except in the case of brief quotations embodied in critical reviews and certain other no commercial uses permitted by copyright law. For permission requests, write to the publisher, addressed "Attention: Permissions Coordinator".

Although the author and publisher have made every effort to ensure that the information in this book was correct at press time, the author and publisher do not assume and hereby disclaim any liability to any party for any loss, injury, damage or disruption caused by errors or omissions, whether such errors or omissions result from negligence, accident, non-functional websites, or any other cause. Any advice or strategy contained herein may not be suitable for every individual.

You may also enjoy:

HOROSCOPE 2015: Astrology and Numerology Horoscopes

The mystery/thrillers:

A Sealed Fate

Holly Leaves

Next of Sin

As well as (all in ebook and paperback):

Delicious, Nutritious Recipes for the Time and Cash Strapped

Paleo Diet: Get Started, Get Motivated, Feel Great. - BESTSELLER

99 ACE Places to Promote Your Book

Pressure Cooking Reinvented. – BEST SELLER

SUGAR FREE DESSERTS WITH PAZAZ - NEW

Weight Loss with the Nordic Diet - NEW

Be Wine Savvy – BEST SELLER

Depression Busters – The Diet to Get you on the Road to Better Mental Health NEW RELEASE

ABOUT THE AUTHOR

Lisa Lazuli studied astrology with the Faculty of Astrological Studies in London.

She has practiced since 1999.

Lisa has been a regular guest on BBWM and BBC Shropshire talking about astrology and doing both horoscopes and live readings. She has also made guest appearances on Fox FM, BBC Cambridgeshire, BBC Northamptonshire, BBC Coventry and Warwickshire and US Internet Radio Shows including the Debra Clement Show.

Lisa wrote horoscopes for Asian Woman Magazine.

Lisa predicted the results of the UK general election 2015.

Now available in eBook and paperback:

TAURUS: Your Day, Your Decan, Your Sign *The most REVEALING book on The Bull yet.* Includes 2015 Predictions.

ARIES HOROSCOPE 2015

TAURUS HOROSCOPE 2015

GEMINI HOROSCOPE 2015

CANCER HOROSCOPE 2015

LEO HOROSCOPE 2015

VIRGO HOROSCOPE 2015

LIBRA HOROSCOPE 2015

SCORPIO HOROSCOPE 2015

SAGITTARIUS HOROSCOPE

CAPRICORN HOROSCOPE 2015

AQUARIUS HOROSCOPE 2015

PISCES HOROSCOPE 2015

Contents

GEMINI 1
  Your Sign, Your Day, Your Decan 1
  Lisa Lazuli 1

GEMINI 11
YOUR DAY YOUR DECAN YOUR SIGN 11
  WORK and INTERESTS 17
  RELATIONSHIPS 21
  HOME LIFE 23
  EMOTIONALLY 25
  HEALTH 25

FIRST DECAN GEMINI 27
SECOND DECAN GEMINI 28
THIRD DECAN GEMINI 30
LOVE MATCHES 33
  GEMINI and ARIES 33
  GEMINI and TAURUS 37
  GEMINI and GEMINI 41
  GEMINI and CANCER 45
  GEMINI and LEO 49
  GEMINI and VIRGO 53
  GEMINI and LIBRA 59
  GEMINI and SCORPIO 63
  GEMINI and SAGITTARIUS 67
  GEMINI and CAPRICORN 71
  GEMINI and AQUARIUS 75
  GEMINI and PISCES 79

YOUR DAY 83
   MAY 21 83
   MAY 22 85
   MAY 23 87
   MAY 24 91
   MAY 25 93
   MAY 26 96
   MAY 27 98
   MAY 28 100
   MAY 29 103
   MAY 30 105
   MAY 31 108
   JUNE 1 111
   JUNE 2 113
   JUNE 3 116
   JUNE 4 119
   JUNE 5 122
   JUNE 6 126
   JUNE 7 128
   JUNE 8 131
   JUNE 10 137
   JUNE 11 140
   JUNE 12 142
   JUNE 13 145
   JUNE 14 148
   JUNE 15 151
   JUNE 16 154
   JUNE 17 157

JUNE 18 160
JUNE 19 163
JUNE 20 165

GEMINI
YOUR DAY YOUR DECAN YOUR SIGN

Gemini - The Twins

Planet – Mercury

Modality – Mutable

Elements – Air

May 21- June 20

Metal – Mercury

Gemstones - Pearl

Number – 5

Rules the Lungs

"I get out of bed at half past ten, I call up my friend who's a party animal."

Gemini love life and they do well at life as they have energy, they like people and are dynamic. Gemini are the party animals of the zodiac as they love to party and tend to have a vibrant and varied social life. Gemini have a wide circle of friends and make friends easily – often many of their friends are somewhat superficial, but as long as they are up for a laugh they are welcome to join the Gemini's circle.

Gemini are great at networking and keeping in touch. They love new gadgets and are bound to be on twitter, Facebook, intsagram and blogging.

They must know what is going on in the world and Gemini are keen followers of current affairs, fashion, new technology and often gossip too. Little escapes their attention and they are insatiably curious.

Gemini are motivated by a quest for knowledge and a search for stimulation and new ideas. Ruled by Mercury, Gemini are changeable and highly adaptable, they have a restless nature and rarely settle to any one thing for long.

They are capable of being objective and highly analytical and it is natural for them to generate ideas and make connections between concepts and also people. Gemini are bright and exciting people to know. They have excellent communication skills and can pick up different languages easily with French often being their favourite. Gemini are mentally orientated and they must be learning, reading or communicating, in fact they find it hard to relax and switch off as their minds are very active. Impatience and the tendency to become distracted can be a big obstacle for Gemini in early life, due to the lure of novelty, something more interesting or just a good time.

Gemini are the messengers of the zodiac and are often found working in journalism and the media which is ideally suited to their personality.

Gemini welcome change and often initiate it in their lives; they get bored quickly and grow out of people and places, which they will leave behind in search of new pastures and opportunities.

They tend to be open to new people and new experiences and this means that the lives of Gemini are filled with variety which is very enjoyable and which others envy. The Twins are quick-witted and sharp mentally and this means that they do well in life regardless of how well they did in school.

Gemini tend to be mentally and physically dexterous and can pick up techniques and skills fast. They are good with their hands and can excel at crafts, trades and arts which require hand to eye co-ordination and skilful use of tools. They are mentally versatile as well and can excel at a variety of disciplines although often they become a jack of all trades master of none as they are less determined when they have to delve into subjects with laborious detail. That said, being an all-rounder is of course a remarkable skill.

Gemini are not suited to routine, mundane and highly detailed work; they work well in fast paced, challenging environments with many people coming and going. Gemini enjoy careers that involve short distance travel i.e. taxi, sales, driving etc.

"I'm in with the in crowd;
I go where the in crowd goes.
I'm in with the in crowd;
And I know what the in crowd knows." – Dobie

Gemini are not loners and must be with people, they are unhappy when alone and feel lost. It is important for Gemini especially in youth to be accepted by a crowd and to this extent they will often go against their own grain to 'fit in' – in later life they are less influenced by peers and the crowd. Gemini take a long while to develop their identity and that identity can change over time as they are chameleons who are actually capable of being different people in different situations. For Gemini identity is not a fixed, highly defined thing, but a concept which is very much related to their growth and the way they change as life leaves its mark on them. Gemini being both mutable and air is the most changeable of all the signs bar Pisces perhaps. This changeability can be seen as fickleness however Gemini live life by being many things to many people.

"When I grow up and want to be a little boy," Joseph Heller.

The twins are known for their youthful appearance, they tend not to age and have a youthful manner and often an even childlike exuberance. Gemini love children, they make excellent educators especially, as they communicate in a lively and entertaining way.

Gemini are highly impressionable and can be influenced strongly by social and cultural factors. Gemini are often called fence sitters as they can have trouble choosing sides because they can see both sides of an argument and they often hold back on nailing their colours to the mast as they wish to retain wriggle room and the right to change their mind – which they often do last minute.

Gemini are terrible procrastinators and can be awful at making a decision unless forced to. Gemini seek to avoid anything which places them in a box or in a corner – they cannot be pigeon holed and labels bounce off them. Gemini dislike confrontation and will usually avoid conflict via their clever wit and ability to talk themselves out of things and side step tricky situations.

Gemini are known as commitment phoebes; they will always think twice before getting tied into anything and yet Gemini crave stability and an anchor and thus marriage suits them well as long as their partner allows them freedom and can laugh, adapt and communicate well.

There is an elusive quality to Gemini; the more you try and grab onto them the more they slip away like a wet soap bar. It can be very hard to fully know or understand a Gemini, many Gemini do not even fully get themselves, but if you are a good listener you will earn the trust of Gemini and they will share their secret fears and beliefs with you.

Gemini often cover up their deep insecurities with humour and constant chatter – one often underestimates how sensitive a Gemini is. Gemini is hurt by coldness and rejection and although they may react with a 'who gives a dam' attitude and even a spiteful comment, they will be affected deeply. Gemini are not hard, this is a sensitive sign, but not necessarily an emotional one. Gemini keep emotions under lock and key and prefer to analyse problems with logic and reason, in fact logic and reason are their key allies in life and what they always turn back to in order make sense of life. Gemini are often confused and perplexed by the highly emotional signs like Scorpio and Pisces – Gemini always feels at sea with the emotional side of life and it can make it very hard for the Gemini to learn what their emotional needs are and how to get them satisfied. Gemini will usually have many significant love relationships – each of which will satisfy and need or a phase in the Gemini's development.

Highly strung, Gemini get irritated very quickly and while they're not angry people and they don't lose their temper, they tend to get irritable when upset. Gemini are emotional chameleons; they adapt to and reflect the mood of the environment they are in. They are the kind of people who seize the moment and live life in the minute. Whether it be at a party or at a sermon, they will have the right words to capture the moment.

Gemini have a love of life and a *joie de vivre* which is intoxicating. Gemini tend to excel at whatever they do at they are thinkers and love to learn.

"Conversation should touch everything but concentrate on nothing," Oscar Wilde.

Gemini love to use their mind they love to rationalise and to categorise things, it is very important for Gemini to understand how things work and how things relate to each other. Speaking and communicating is a vital to Gemini nature and the way they learn to understand themselves and make sense of what is going on in their lives. Gemini are able to hold two opposing views in their heads at the same time without fear of contradiction – they like to keep an open mind they will rarely commit to one thing exclusively.

Gemini are not a canvas but a movie – something that changes and goes through phases, always moving forward and always developing. Gemini can appear unreliable due to this ability to change life course or opinion in the light of new information, but it is the key to their survival and success. Gemini never get bogged down in their own dogma.

An obsessive need to dart from thing to thing and never miss out on anything can take its toll on the Gemini nerves and many Gemini suffer stress and need to find ways of winding down and getting to a point of total relaxation. Gemini often burn the candle at both ends and can be incredibly hard workers who keep going until late in life: Joan Rivers was still working at 82 and still fit as a gazelle when she died (due to a throat op gone wrong). Paul McCartney, Jackie Mason, Barry Manilow and Tom Jones are other Geminis still going in the tough showbiz world into their 70's – Gemini have amazing longevity. Prince Phillip, Duke of Edinburgh (HRH) is a Gemini and at almost 100 years old is still doing a full schedule of engagements with a smile and his distinctive brand of humour.

Gemini are lively and entertaining and are a welcome addition to any social group; they make friends fast and are good at keeping in touch and arranging get togethers. Gemini are great improvisers and can rescue situations by being crafty and using words carefully. Gemini are extremely clever with words and how to use them and this makes them great speech writers, copy writers, newspaper headline writers and spin doctors. Often Gemini are accused of talking from both sides of their mouth with a car-salesman slickness and it is true that some Gemini lack integrity and can play lose and fast with facts. Gemini are not in general dishonest but they can use the sugar coating of words to conceal a multitude of sins.

"If you can't baffle them with brilliance, then befuddle them with bullshit!" Anon

Gemini can be slapdash and enjoy doing everything as fast as possible, accuracy is often sacrificed for speed. Gemini are supple and thus make good dancers and gymnasts. Gemini are forever young and get on very well with children; in a way, the mischievous child lives inside every Gemini who also enjoy jokes and prank playing.

WORK and INTERESTS

Gemini don't have the best concentration and although they are enthusiastic learners, they often make poor scholars as they find regimented study boring. Gemini do far better where they can learn by doing as they pick things up very quickly: they are excellent at conceptualising and working through problems. Gemini are thirsty for knowledge, the one drawback however is that they often talk too much and listen too little.

Gemini have a great capacity to learn and challenging ideas and concepts are no problem for them. Gemini hate routine, they love variety and enjoy being spontaneous. Gemini are known for being inventive and innovative and they are drawn to positions where they can write, experiment or criticise.

Gemini must have change as well as intellectual and social stimulation in their work. They enjoy movement and relish jobs which enable them to travel locally or internationally or indeed jobs involving transport or travel.

Geminis are often involved in the exchange of information or logistical matters. Gemini are also born educators and conveyors of information and news which is why so many become journalists or news writers. Gemini are especially prominent in the modern media and are experts at exploiting social media.

With a knack of getting on with others they thrive in people orientated businesses. Gemini also make good translators, interpreters and foreign language teachers.

They enjoy work in sales and are great at conveying facts about products and showing enthusiasm for what they sell. They do well in careers which involve quite a bit of talking.

The Twins make good teachers and child minders as they enjoy working with children; they must still however have adequate adult conversation.

They are great readers and love newspapers. Mental games and games of skill appeal to Gemini; they enjoy chess, puzzles and sports like tennis, cricket, baseball, fencing, table tennis, squash and badminton.

Gemini needs periods of rest interspersed with periods of activity to get the most out of themselves.

Gemini can excel at many careers due to their versatility however they do best where there is change and new stimulus on a daily basis – 'new' being the operative word as Gemini love what is NEW, be it fashion, current affairs or gadgets.

Gemini have excellent reasoning ability and can work well where there is a need to be unbiased and impartial and see facts without emotions interfering with the thought process. Gemini can look at facts coldly and disparagingly without being swayed, although they can still take a long while to come to a conclusion. Some Gemini do well in scientific fields in terms of coming up with ideas, they rarely have the patience for the long years of R&D needed to bring a product to market.

Gemini value education and aim to have a wide spectrum of knowledge covering culture to sports; they often have an excellent vocabulary and know how to communicate with great effect. Many Gemini are highly sophisticated and can be very intimidating as they can come up with facts and figures fast giving the impression that they know a subject very well – often they are blagging it, but they always give the impression of knowledge.

Remember when your teacher said that you couldn't do two things at once (i.e. talk to friends in class and learn), well if you are Gemini she was wrong. Gemini can multi task and find it quite possible to do two things simultaneously. Watch TV while writing an essay; hold a meeting while trading stocks online…why not? Gemini function well in complex and fast paced environments, but they must never ignore their need to get away from it, take a proper breather and relax to restore your frazzled nerves, preventing fatigue and

18

exhaustion. Gemini cannot deny the importance of periods of seclusion.

Gemini are very impatient and can be rather irritable when confronted by obstacles and hiccoughs – they need to develop more patience and endurance skills.

Intensely curious Gemini want to know the ins and out of things and yet they can lose interest quite quickly. They are quick to join groups and causes or try sports but often they do not stay the pace, jumping instead to the next fad. In fact Gemini's are often criticised for being fad-tastic. Gemini love jokes, cartoons and poetry as well as satire.

Gemini travel more for pleasure than business and are partial to mixing the two.

On the negative side, some Gemini can descend into talking incessantly about matters of no consequence, achieving little and dealing in gossip and hearsay. In some cases Gemini may skirt about the periphery issues, not having the strength to address the core issues at stake.

Sometimes Gemini shirk responsibility and look for the easy way out in matters that become a little fraught.

Gemini usually have big families and get on well with siblings.

RELATIONSHIPS

Gemini allow their head to rule in matters of the heart and will look to evaluate potential partners according to logic and reason. They place a great value on friendship in relationships and prefer rapport to passion. They must have a partner who is stimulating, enjoys talking and likes to try new things. It is preferable for Gemini to team up with someone who enjoys nightlife or entertaining. Friends and events are going to be part of the Gemini life and so the partner must be up for it: homebodies need not apply.

Gemini are big flirts and a partner must be strong enough to laugh this off and to realise that this is their nature. Gemini will play the field and like to see what is out there and experience different types of relationships before settling down. Gemini love variety in their social life and they are curious about people which makes them want to get close to a range of people – thus they are unlikely to settle down to a permanent relationship. Gemini also struggle to make up their minds and are often faced with choosing between two possible partners. Gemini cannot be forced into a corner and ultimatums and deadlines in love drive them away. Gemini are capable of sustained commitment to the right person.

Gemini are always looking for the other half, a soul mate to fill that gap and make them feel whole. Gemini often feel incomplete and with that can come insecurity; that is why they seek understanding and emotional fulfilment in relationships. Gemini like to be listened to – they cannot stand vagueness and need to get a feeling they are truly understood. Gemini are good listeners and need to be with good listeners.

The Gemini tendency to analyse and almost turn relationships into business flowcharts or psychoanalyse can be frustrating and annoying for signs who think more emotionally and who rely on heart, feel and gut instinct.

Gemini will resent people who try and pin them down and control them – they are people who become evasive and closed when confronted with bossy, domineering types.

Gemini make cheerful, tolerant, bubbly and amusing companions, but their feelings fluctuate which can make those with them insecure and confused.

Gemini dislike what is coarse or rough and will seek refined, well-mannered and informed people as partners.

HOME LIFE

Gemini like to ring the changes and when you visit their homes you will be amazed as things will have changed from the last time you visited – new cushions, curtains, walls repainted a trendy colours and decor rearranged. Gemini like to throw the older things out and get in something more modern and fresh. They hate clutter and like the surfaces and tables to be clear. Their book shelves are full and they do like mementos from their travels.

Conversation and drinks will flow and sometimes the food burns as you are all so busy chatting. Gemini will love to impress you with their culinary skills and ability to serve Jamie Oliver's or Gordon Ramsay's latest delight. Gemini are adventurous with food and prefer trying new things to old fashioned recipes: Floyd on Food was Gemini. Gemini are not natural cooks, but like any other subject they like to try and when entertaining will make an effort even if they normally have a TV dinner. Gemini will delight in showing you the latest films or showing you the latest gadgets in their kitchen – they must have a modern, ergonomic kitchen. Gemini enjoy tiles and wooden floors rather than carpet and they are not fans of chintz. You will get to bed very late when visiting a Gemini

Gemini enjoy their children and make for fun parents who take an active interest in their child's schooling. Gemini can however let themselves become too discombobulated by all the latest child care fads that they wonder what to do next. Gemini find their children keep them young and in touch which of course is very important to them. They worry quite a bit about getting parenting 'right' and are quick to make changes and listen to advice. Gemini make friends of their kids and their kids friends and are cool parents.

EMOTIONALLY

Gemini benefit from learning new skills and training their minds; they need to feel engaged with the world and fully involved in life – Gemini never like to live on the edges, they want to be in the centre.

Gemini must be able to express themselves in relationships and must feel that they are listened to. Relationships where communication is one way cannot fulfil a Gemini emotionally. Gemini must be able to talk out problems and cannot tolerate prolonged silences and estrangement without on ongoing exchange of some sort.

It can be hard for Gemini to establish meaningful and emotionally fulfilling connections with others, often they just behave like social butterflies touching base with all and sundry and never actually connecting with anyone.

When unfulfilled or insecure emotionally Gemini can become lost in a superficial existence, scattering energy and cultivating relationships with people who are not capable of giving you what you really need. Intellectual pursuits can often become a refuse from emotional loneliness.

HEALTH

Gemini rules the hands, shoulder, arms and lungs. As I have already mentioned, restlessness and anxiety plague Gemini as they find it hard to switch off and relax.

Most commonly Gemini suffer from insomnia and the related problem of anxiety. Gemini tend to come down with illness when they are stressed out, which is probably the only way your body can give you the message that you need to slow down. Gemini neglect their diet and eat a load of rubbish when they are busy and on the go and this can run you down further, making you vulnerable to illness.

the arms and shoulders and internally the lungs, ...s, nerves fibres, bronchus and trachea. Gemini may be ...ble to bronchitis and pneumonia, so they need to take care of themselves during colds so they do not develop into chest infections. Gemini may also suffer from allergies, asthma, anaemia and eczema.

Other problems which may affect Gemini are arthritis, carpel tunnel syndrome and poor circulation. Tension tends to be felt in the lungs and may worsen asthma. Calming therapies and techniques should be attempted and evaluated as they can revolutionise the Gemini health. Regular and varied exercise can be really helpful as Gemini do get bored with regimented and onerous exercise regimes.

Gemini should eat vegetables that contain potassium chloride i.e. asparagus, green beans, tomato, celery, carrots, spinach, oranges, peaches, apricots, plums and wild rice. Other helpful fruits, veg and food stuffs are: grapefruit, almonds, shellfish, broiled fish, apples and raisins.

Moderation is vital and the Gemini can improve health with more consistency rather than by going from one fad to another.

Lettuce and cucumber are vital for Gemini who have chest and lung issues.

FIRST DECAN GEMINI

May 22 to May 31

Ruled by Mercury

Intelligent, talkative and high versatile. First Decan Gemini are highly savvy and exhibit Gemini traits to a tee. You are inquisitive and enjoy communicating and exchanging ideas – you may well be an educator, lecturer, publisher or writer as you love putting information out there especially on topics that are HOT. You are less likely to have an interest in writing on history, geography, history of art or subjects that are not currently evolving or progressing.

You have a constant raging battle between head and heart: your emotions and your desire for reasoning and logic will pull you in different directions. You are more comfortable with things that add up and make sense and less likely to trust feelings and instincts; however when your head tells you one thing and your heart another you can feel very confused and this can set you off balance and make you delay acting or encourage you to avoid acting or making a decision altogether. You generally go with your head when it comes to it and it can make you seem cold at times when others are anticipating you making a more sentimental or emotionally driven decision.

You are both articulate and witty and make for a very entertaining companion and colleague. You make friends fast and have a wide social network and yet it can be harder for you to develop deeper close friendships; in one way you enjoy the fulfilment a relationship with a more intense person can offer and yet when you do get very close to anyone you feel trapped and look for a way out. In a way you repel what you really want, due to your restless nature and desire for freedom. It takes a very special combination of passion yet distance to satisfy and not scare off a Gemini first decan. You must have freedom and you need someone to respect you and love you, but never to ask too many questions or set too many rules. Trust is a BIG DEAL for you – giving it and getting it.

You are a perfectionist and can be rather demanding. You are critical of others and have a sharp mind for facts and figures – even if figures are not your thing you will still be sharp with money and will watch deals and transactions like a hawk to ensure they go well. You are astute in business and also negotiations. Anyone who takes you for a fool, is indeed the bigger fool. Gemini 1st decan were not born yesterday. Earl to bed early to rise – they catch the worm.

Liberal and humanitarian these Gemini like to be involved in social and humanitarian causes.

SECOND DECAN GEMINI

June 1 to June 11

Ruled by Venus

Charming, affable, easy going and sociable. You have a wonderful way about you which helps you to win friends and influence people: a charismatic communicator and creative thinker. You enjoy spreading joy and excitement and you are a natural entertainer.

You have the ability to achieve your aims due to your ability to deftly handle situations and people; you can be very persuasive and can sway opinion by appealing to people's logic. You are someone who brings others together and helps foster cooperation and harmony.

An eye for beauty, shape and form mean that you can be very successful in artistic fields and graphic design. Your versatility and ability to get on with people can mean that you will be very successful in any people orientated work environment. Your worst enemy is a tendency to laziness and taking the easy way out – you can sometimes not have the guts to tell people to their face what you say behind their back. You do not like to be the bearer of bad news in fact you often avoid difficult conversations.

You are well suited to the arts, marketing, sales of beauty products and consumer goods and retail.

You are a great entertainer and thrive amongst people – you can also do well in the hospitality industry. You are a great host and love to entertain – your home is open doors for friends and family. You are very inclusive and like to make everyone feel at home – you are rarely angry or nasty. Little flusters you and you like to go with the flow. You need to develop more aggression in competitive situations as you may lack a certain degree of commitment when things get tough.

Do not be a soft touch – know your boundaries and defend them with more vigour. You can be quite erratic in that you go from determined and driven to totally scatty and comme ci comme ca – who knows what to expect? You love to make others happy, but you should not allow this to totally distract you or overwhelm you.

You are capable of being fair and objective and can be a talented adjudicator and judge. Highly considerate, you work very well in teams and partnerships. Your health is always improved by being in peaceful and beautiful environments – negativity can have an adverse effect on your nerves. You can create a beautiful life for yourself by eliminating negative thoughts and cultivating loving, harmonious thought and affirmations.

The law of attraction works well for Gemini 2nd decans who benefit from good karma.

You are very involved in relationships and forming close, lasting attachments matter to you. You take relationships and matters of the heart more seriously than the other decans and dislike being single. You will sacrifice some freedom for closeness as you dislike being alone.

THIRD DECAN GEMINI

Ruled by Uranus

June 12 – June 20

A dramatic, original decan of Gemini who demand to be noticed.

Extremely outspoken and restless. You love mental challenges and excel at maths and science. You are inventive and often quite radical in your thinking. Progressive and ready to embrace new things, you are a mover and shaker.

You are known for your originality and even genius – you are at the forefront of new ideas and concepts. You are an intellectual firebrand giving leadership especially in alternate or cutting edge subjects. You can bring little known subjects into the mainstream and make them more accessible.

You may well work with technology, electricity or scientific fields especially those related to communications, energy and transport. You are controversial and can be very direct. Original and never restrained by convention you are bound to be anti-establishment. Your life will be filled with the unexpected and quite a bit of excitement. You are very positive and optimistic and see life as an adventure where risks should be taken – nothing much holds you back. You are a rebel and resist any restraints. You are a charmer which means that no matter how crazy your ideas sound you can win support.

Your unconventional thoughts can sometimes isolate you, but you are not an approval seeker – you enjoy sparking controversy. You love to be involved and have a very active mind. This decan is very vulnerable in terms of their nerves and yoga or meditation for relaxation is vital.

You thrive on freedom and fast paced activity – you hate being constrained and do not fare well in regimented environments. Boredom is your biggest fear and also your biggest obstacle in life –

you bore of things fast and that means you do not always complete on your projects as you may lack concentration, staying power and the ability to see things through when they going gets tough.

The Chinese have a saying, "A decision mad in haste is a bad one," hasty decisions and throwing the baby out with the bathwater can also wreck the excellent plans of this decan.

A decan of great intelligence and ideas, however the ability to organise and manage people and resources may be lacking. You work best where you have autonomy and can be creative and inventive. You work in bursts and energy can come and go. Lack of moderation can be a thorn in your side.

This decan is highly intuitive and often attracted to the occult and scientific fields – anything where there is opportunity for higher understanding. Alternate therapies, new age thought and research are often areas this decan pour their energy into. You have the ability to sense things which can be hard to understand logically. You may teach others difficult subjects as you can make them more accessible.

Tradition is often rejected in favour of modern ways. This decan is all about the future not the past.

This decan can be totally indifferent to anything which does not interest or excite them – they often make up their minds to dislike something, someone or some concept and can be scathing about that concept or person. They can have strong political views. While you love change, you can be somewhat stubborn about certain beliefs you have.

A life of sometimes drastic and sudden changes – learning lessons from experience is vital. You often jump from the frying pan to the fire as you are impulsive and do not always plan – however often things work out really well.

LOVE MATCHES

GEMINI and ARIES

Cardinal FIRE and Mutable AIR = Hurricane

Two POSITIVE SIGNS.

Gemini burn the candle at both ends and Aries is the accelerant.

Sparks will fly right away and there is an immediate attraction; this relationship will get off to a quick start. It will be exciting and full of spontaneity and excitement.

Aries find Gemini fun and exciting and the Gemini enjoys the way Aries dives right in and gets the ball rolling. Aries initiate and the Gemini goes along with enthusiasm. Aries says, 'Let's do this' and Gemini says, "This is how!"

Both have an almost childlike enthusiasm for life and both are un-cynical and happy to believe the best in people – both can be naive. These are optimists who look forward not back and do not dwell on things.

Both like surprises and Aries loves the Gemini's jokes and sense of fun – these two can get into trouble together, although it's the Aries who may get the blame as Gemini are slick talkers, good at choosing the right words to avoid trouble. This is a paring with no brakes – hence problems stopping what you start.

Aries have more physical stamina and may tire out the Gemini; but Gemini will exhaust the Arian with their constant chatter. These two can both burn the candle at both ends and in the middle.

They make terrific friends and as colleagues they can spur each other on to make great achievements.

There will be plenty of activity in this relationship; nights out, entertaining friends and weekends away. But, how will it fair in the longer run? Air and fire equal hot air and sometimes that is what this couple generate - plenty of hot air and no real substance.

Despite astrology texts which will tell you this is a good combination, in the long run this combination will be unlikely to last unless both have a strong earth influence. This will go well until you move in together or get married, when the problems will start. Aries can be too bossy for Gemini who prefer to go with the flow, Aries tend to be more regimented and can quite like structure. Aries are pushy at times and like to corner Gemini; who immediately feel like they are being boxed in and coerced. Aries, once in stable relationship can lose their spontaneity, and may even become homebodies, while the Gemini still wants to be fancy free and get out and about.

Both signs love children and so family life will be on the cards and yet the approach to childrearing can be very different – Aries can be strict and will encourage the child to yield to authority, while the Gemini will want to be the child's friend and peer. Could be a good cop, bad cop style of parenting. The Gemini parent want the child to be well read and will focus on education; the Aries will encourage the child to be competitive and to stand up for itself – both will foster independence.

Gemini are uncomfortable with Aries' more aggressive side. Gemini recoil from confrontation and when Aries lose their temper they want to get as far away as possible. Aries like to have things out in the open, where Gemini are masters of avoidance. Aries have strong ideas about how things should be done and are less flexible and often less progressive than Gemini – who are much more adaptable and like to go with the flow. Aries react with gut feel and Gemini like to think rationally; instinct and intuition are Aries's key allies while Gemini much prefer to trust logic and reason – this can mean they do not often understand each other.

Aries can often get drawn into missions, where they get sucked into long and often exhausting battles – Gemini can find this highly frustrating. Gemini like to argue and talk things out, where Aries fly off the handle and say whatever comes to mind and want Gemini to forgive and forget after wards. Gemini can be hurt by the bluntness of the Aries and Aries seems totally unaware of Gemini's more sensitive nature. Gemini may feel misunderstood and as I have said, being understood is vital to their self-esteem.

Aries like to act and act fast; they strike while the iron is hot and Gemini's indecisiveness is very aggravating for them. Aries get a feeling and go with it; Gemini prefer to hold back and think about things – they find Aries too reactionary and feel they shoot from the hip.

The aggression and domineering side of Aries can drive Gemini away and the evasiveness of Gemini is upsetting for Aries. The more Aries tries to direct the relationship, the more Gemini drifts away. These two will argue quite a bit and often there is not enough to bring them together again. Friendships between these two can also suffer as they may drift off in different directions or argue and never really have the impetus to patch things up.

Aries are competitive and sometime this desire to be first can ware on Gemini; in a similar way Gemini's ability to out-argue and mentally side step the Aries can frustrate the Aries. Aries are never fully sure if they can trust Gemini and their flirtatious actions offend the Arian who may feel they are being shown up.

This is a very unstable combination as both Aries are volatile and Gemini are changeable – you will have your ups and downs and times apart. Work, social life and projects will often pull you in different directions and finding time together to devote to nurturing your relationship may be last on the list. This combination lacks stability and also passion – you can take each other for-granted.

This astrological pairing is more successful as friends or as one off friends with benefits (if that is how you like to roll).

Both of you are very active people and so your sex life will be active and very spontaneous – kitchen sink, garden, nowhere is outta bounds. Both of you get bored quickly and this is was causes a drive for constant change and novelty which can actually drive you apart eventually. Gemini find conversation stimulating and can actually get quite sexual after a good debate or in depth discussion. Intelligence turns Gemini on and Aries have to make more of an effort to be good listeners and communicators to get the most from Gemini. Aries can find too much talk boring and they want to get on with it, a balance need to be sought.

Sexually there is plenty of adventure and excitement which can be rather inspiring for both – you both like to try new things and to improve your sexual experiences. Neither of you hold back. The fun factor is well up the scale, but in terms of loving and affection neither of you have time for laying in the afterglow for long.

These two may date on and off for years and never get to the commitment stage.

This combination works better with the 2nd Decan Gemini who can calm and soothe the Arian and there will be more romance and a deeper friendship. Friendship, not romance is more likely with 3rd Decan Geminis, but heated arguments are likely. Relationships with 1st Decan Gemini wont' last long.

This works well while you are both living for the moment – so good for young lovers and older folks with no family ties. Not a combo that deals well with day to day responsibilities and routines. It can run hot and cold and this combo gives neither of you stability and security.

Famous Aries-Gemini Couples: Charlie Chaplin and Paulette Goddard, Warren Beatty and Annette Bening

GEMINI and TAURUS

Fixed EARTH and Mutable AIR = Sand Storms

How will the solid Taurean handle the fickle Gemini. How will free spirited, changeable Gemini put up with the stick in the mud Bull?

Taurus finds the changeable dual nature of the Twins confusing and the Bull also finds Gemini's whimsical affection comes and goes and the flirting drives the Bull into a rage.

This can be a combination that works, but there are certainly problems and issues that arise. Taurus finds Gemini exciting and beguiling; the Twins open the Bull's pastures up and the Bulls learns news things, tries new things and thinks about new things.

Both highly sociable signs who enjoy people and socialising these two will have great fun dating. Taurus loves theatre, dining out, movies, concerts, sports games and Gemini are very happy to go along as they love to know what's hot and what's going on. Gemini will introduce Taurus to many new people and expand the social circle of the Bull which goes down well. Both Gemini and Taurus are great networkers and so businesswise they work well together.

This relationship has great promise in the beginning as both are intrigued and in awe of each other. Taurus loves the spontaneity, the spark and the wit of the Gemini; while Gemini loves the warmth, the kindness, the genuine nature and the sense of humour of the Bull.

Taurus can give Gemini an anchor and make him/her feel secure and stronger; Gemini love the solid advice and reassurance of the Bull. Gemini bring more fun, novelty and conversation into the Taureans life – he/she is interesting and makes life seem less black and white.

Gemini live in the moment and can help Taurus to do the same especially in love making. Playful and experimental in love Gemini help Taurus to try new things and the Bull brings warmth and fire to the sexual arena, exposing the Gemini to more on a sensual and touch level.

The problem comes later in the relationship: in the long term Taurus are concerned about seeing commitment and getting ever closer to the other; the excitement of the playfulness and teasing wear off. The problem is as the relationship progresses: the Bull tries to get ever closer and the freedom loving Gemini just keeps slipping away. The Bull cannot come to terms with the manner in which he/she cannot 'possess' the Twins. The Bull may become tired of his/her friends and may actually resent them. The Bull may find that the Gemini is not deep enough for him and the Gemini may find the Bull too controlling and too intent on being ubiquitous.

Taurus takes the Gemini's changing moods to heart and tries to read too much into his/her words; Gemini want Taurus to take life less seriously. Gemini have a hard time with the Bull's feelings as the Bull can be touchy; the Bull gets irritated with the Gemini indecisiveness and the way she/he likes to do things on the spur of the moment. Taurus used to love the spur of the moment stuff when they dated and yet now he/she finds it more trouble than it's worth. The Bull can find the Twins insincere and false and he prefers honesty and wants to be him/herself, who gives a dam about superficial stuff and appearances. Gemini may feel trapped in the relationship and as if they are stagnating. The more the Bull senses a lack of commitment the more possessive he/she becomes.

The Gemini needs to be more affectionate and knows that the Bull wants to hear the words, "I love you!" The Taurus needs to allow the Gemini more freedom and must be more tolerant. You each have qualities the other lack and can learn from each other, however you need to be open to learning and willing to change and grow or you will simply clash.

Gemini have the ability to help the Bull uncover hidden talents and potentials; the Gemini is always encouraging him/her to try new things and can be very supportive and helpful. The Gemini says a lot and the Bull needs to listen more and take things on board. The ideas of the Gemini can be very helpful to the Taurus in business and money-wise this combination works very well for Taurus. The Bull can be financially prosperous with a Gemini.

The Bull is very upfront and always appreciates the way Gemini talks about everything, he never has to guess as the twins are great communicators. Taurus however have this nagging feeling that the Twins are very clever with words and that they do re-mix the truth on occasion, leading the Bull to believe he/she can never fully trust the Gemini mate.

The Bull can help the Gemini be more in touch with his/her inner self and to come to terms with deeply buried issues. Being with the Bull makes the Gemini feel everything is possible and he/she develops confidence and more of a sense of self. Via knowing the Bull a Gemini can achieve more self-honesty and will get to know and understand him/herself better; Gemini will tend to have time to think more and to see things differently.

Often introduced by mutual friends, this can be a very good pairing for growth and for each to develop new skills, abilities and unused character traits. The strength of the Bull can give the Gemini a solid platform from which to succeed and the versatility and mental abilities, sharpness and wit of the Gemini will help Taurus to keep learning, keep innovating and think things through better.

This combo is exciting and entertaining for both. There will be arguments and even break ups, but you cannot deny you need and love each other and just have to work things through as you go and compromise.

Works even better when Taurus is on: 23 April or 5, 14 May.

Or when the Gemini is on: 24 May, 2, 6, 11, 15, 20 June.

Queen Elizabeth (Taurus) and Prince Phillip (Gemini)

Emilio Estevez (Taurus) and Paul Abdul (Gemini) – Divorced

Andre Agassi (Taurus) and Steffi Graff (Gemini)

GEMINI and GEMINI

Mutable AIR x 2 = Tornados

Sparks will fly; the attraction is immediate and you are going to be whipping up a storm conversation-wise. This combination also works well with age gap relationships.

Gemini love other Gemini in terms of friendship and hit it off right away.

Communication is the name of the game with Gemini and so you can easily satisfy this need in each other – however are either of you really listening properly? You may also over talk and over analyse things which could do more to make mountains out of molehills than resolving things. Gemini are symbolised by the Twins and in many ways you may be Karmic twins in terms of the way you connect. This combination works well with 2 second decan Gemini or a 2nd and 1st Decan, as the emotional and physical side is far deeper and more satisfying. Two 1st decan Gemini can clash especially when the ego is involved – you both want intellectual superiority. 1st or 2nd Decan Gemini can bond with 3rd Decan Gemini on a very spiritual level and this deeper, almost karmic connection can make the problems that arise easier to get beyond.

Gemini enjoy the intellectual side of relationships and like to be stimulated mentally; they cannot fall for someone who is silent, unwilling to engage and distant and this is why two Gemini click. You are both social and will enjoy each other's friends and going out to theatre and events – this love of life and interest in what's new and what's going on really keeps your relationship interesting. You will talk about everything from politics to gossip about the neighbours.

Gemini deal in ideas and they look at things conceptually more than emotionally and that can mean that you are able to discuss matters within the relationship and sexually in a constructive way.

Both are creative and inventive and you make a dynamic couple – you can be very effective in business as a team especially in sales, marketing and social media.

What this relationship does lack is stability. Neither of you is a safe container for the other; the 1st and 2nd of the Gemini decans have no earthy element in particular and are very changeable. There is no anchor here and also no glue – the question is what will actually keep you together in the long term?

This relationship also lacks moderation and can be haphazard; neither of you are planners and there is a manana manana or 'life happens while you are making other plans' syndrome. Every relationship has to have the one who holds the other's hair back while they vomit; the one that holds the handbag while the other goes on the big dipper and the one who makes the shopping list and balances the cheque book – Gemini with Gemini can lack that person.

Dealing with routines, creating structure and financial planning is not the Gemini's favourite thing. Gemini are often great at making money, but managing it is another thing and with two Geminis it will be up to one to take responsibility and take the adult role. When Real Life strikes this partnership can struggle. That is why an age gap helps as you are at different stages of life and the older one can add maturity and wisdom.

Neither of you are hung up on details and it may well be that you skirt around issues both emotional and sexual without getting to the nitty gritty. Gemini often say a lot, but say very little – Gemini are quite shy in broaching certain heavier topics. This pairing need to build the emotional understanding within the relationship for both of your benefit; this can take effort and also commitment. Make sure you give each other your undivided attention at least once a day as Gemini's minds are often on more than one thing at a time and yet when it comes to love you want your partner to be all ears.

A Gemini may understand another Gemini only superficially and the relationship could be one of those that lives on the surface, which is quite adequate but which always feels lacking. "Doing all right but not very well!"

Sexually this relationship is great, but the great sex only lasts once committed if you do work on the love and affection part of the deal. Two commitment shy Gemini – will you ever get down the aisle? If you are together for a long while it may be more down to fluke than design. In fact Gemini Gemini last well when you take it a day at a time – forcing yourselves into some structured arrangement may be the death knell.

This pair will have some superb memories no matter how things end; in fact they can still be friends after a relationship/marriage ends. Your strengths and weaknesses will be magnified by this combination which can mean a huge variety of experience, but also stress from being mentally over taxed. Jealousy and possessiveness are not likely to be issues, but you will compete with each other intellectually – this may push you on to great achievements in your job. You'll talk long into the night and will not get that much sleep. Your changeability and erratic nature will not throw another Gemini off kilter.

Many Gemini Gemini will have affairs – this reflects the spontaneous and rather risqué element both love.

This can last especially if one or the other have a strong Saturn or earth planets.

Famous Gemini-Gemini Couples: Barbara and George Walker Bush, Shia La Boeuf and Carey Mulligan.

GEMINI and CANCER

Mutable AIR and Cardinal WATER = Tidal Wave Energy

The fluctuating emotional nature of Cancer is both confounding and disconcerting for Gemini, who are never quite sure where they are. Both these signs are changeable, but for different reasons and the Gemini irritability and Cancerian moodiness can make for choppy waters. Gemini understand things by logic and deduction and Cancer are highly intuitive and guided by instinct – thus when it comes to decision making they are coming at it from very different angles which can actually be very helpful and instructive to them both. These signs compliment and balance each other and since both have a degree of flexibility they should yield to and learn from the other.

Cancer are sensitive and so are Gemini, however Gemini conceals their sensitivity and both are hurt by very different things: thus it can be hard for them not to put their foot in it occasionally.

Cancer are extremely motivated people and they can help Gemini put more action and effort into their plans. Cancer provide leadership and direction to this relationship. It may well be the Cancer who initiates and keep things going in the early stages of the relationship in particular.

Gemini are ruled by the head and Cancer are ruled by their emotions – they make decisions about their life, friendships and relationships on the basis of an emotional pull which they follow unquestioningly. Gemini must know the whys and wherefores of everything and they find the Cancerian's decision making process baffling. You feel very differently about things and while a Gemini analyses a Cancerian goes with instinct and rarely looks back.

These two will have to be thrust together so that they can get to know each other as they are not likely to strike up a convo at a club and hit it off that way. There are obvious hurdles to overcome and 3rd Decan Gemini will be unlikely to match with a Cancer. This relationship grows over time and does require that you accept and respect your differences – the problem is you are more likely to want to change each other.

Both of you are very driven and as long as you both pursue your own interests and have strong individual goals this should bode well for the relationship. The biggest hurdle for this pair is joint decision making over issues that concern you both i.e. home, finances and family. Cancer can however help Gemini develop business and financial management skills and also encourage Gemini to be more determined. You do well together when you divide up and concentrate on what you are both best at.

Cancer are a cautious sign and Gemini like to try new things with a sense of adventure; Cancerians may wince at the Gemini carelessness and the Gemini may find the Cancerian a wet blanket. Cancer can be a little negative and when they are hurt and upset they retreat and will not talk; this can drive the Gemini mad as they want to have it out and reason with the crab. The Cancerian moodiness and need to be alone is hard for the Gemini to deal with.

Cancerians are homebodies at heart and like to settle down; Gemini are not the settling down kind and for them the new out is definitely not IN.

Cancerians strangely enough do understand Gemini – they perhaps understand Gemni better than they understand themselves – but this can become uncomfortable for the Gemini. The Cancerian really cares and will offer advice, but Gemini will feel bossed around. Cancer may become manipulative and possessive using emotional leverage to get power within the relationship – the Cancer holds all the cards.

Cancer are ambitious and socially mobile; they may fell Gemini don't always play the game or take their aims seriously enough.

There may be a lack of team work when it comes to what the Cancer feels are future plans for the family.

Gemini like to talk in the bedroom and the Cancer like massage and physical intimacy with less of the talk. Cancer is skilled at non-verbal communication and at picking up subtle signs; Gemini are less subtle, but can learn from the Cancer if they can just relax and concentrate. Again there is much to be learned and for personal development this is great combination, but is there the will to do this learning?

Famous Gemini-Cancer Couples: Nicole Kidman and Tom Cruise, Wallace Simpson and the Duke of Windsor, Jessica Tandy and Hume Cronyn.

GEMINI and LEO

Mutable AIR and FIXED Fire = BURNOUT

Two spontaneous fun loving signs who will hit it off fast, but who may tire each other out. You value fun and playfulness in love to a degree that is almost childlike – but love should make us feel young! Gemini are flirts and they love to maintain a wide social circle; the Leo can feel slightly threatened by this as Leo like to be put on a pedestal and they do not like to feel there is competition. Leo, as a fixed sign needs certainly and loyalty and somehow Gemini can never quite convince a Leo that they are loyal and committed. Leo like to be centre of attention and Gemini have a short attention span.

Gemini is the one who laughs things off, but Leo can sulk after arguments and Leo can take a while to come round again, however there is something irresistible about the Gemini which the Leo cannot stay away from for long.

The communication between you flows like a broadband superhighway, which is appreciated by both of you who are highly expressive. Both these signs are creative and energetic which makes for a couple who love going places and doing things. Settling down and having kids can lead to changes in the very foundation of the relationship which is – FUN. Suddenly there is responsibility and you are both more tied down; the partner who feels more tied down (i.e. the primary caregiver) may feel resentful of the partner who still has some degree of freedom. That said, you both love children and so the motivation to have them is very high and you will enjoy bringing them up and both of you will encourage them to be outgoing and fully engaged in activities.

Sometimes the Leo need for security in the relationship can come across as jealousy or possessiveness and nothing drives the Gemini away faster than a partner who shows signs of being controlling. Gemini need freedom and need a partner to understand their need to have many relationships. Not all Gemini relationships mean something and Leo need to understand that. Leo need to be more secure in themselves and realise they may be projecting insecurity outwards and blaming the Gemini. Gemini need to express their emotions more demonstratively to the Leo. If Leo cannot get to a point of trust then they can become increasingly dramatic and the Gemini can become more and more evasive which drives them apart. The Gemini does not understand the Leo nature's needs for intensity and that anger is just a part of their passion; for a Gemini love is about talking and communicating, never being angry. Consistency and routine is far more important to the Leo than it is to Gemini; the Leo may find Gemini's constant need for variety draining and superficial – in fact the Lion may want the Gemini to change and settle down at some point.

In the main this is a positive pairing which lends itself to a relationship full of variety and sexual excitement. The Leo can give the Gemini a boost in confidence and provide a stability which can help the Gemini focus on goals. The Leo is secretly very sensitive as is the Gemini and once they learn that about each other they can have great mutual respect for each others' feelings. They can easily satisfy each other's sexual, intellectual and also their emotional needs; but the emotional side needs more maturity from both of you for it to work.

Leo's way is to dominate and take control and Gemini may find that they come on too strong – you may always be one upping each other or trying to outdo the other, this can be exhausting or it can propel you both to great achievement. You need to accept that there are different areas where you excel and then allow each other to shine in those areas without competing.

Leo's love will make the Gemini feel that their talents and personality are appreciated – Leos like to take centre stage, but they like to trumpet others too and they will encourage the Gemini talents. You are both social animals and if you work in similar fields there are great networking opportunities by being together. Leo can be hard task masters and are very fixed in terms of their thinking; the Gemini are more mentally adaptable and respond quicker to change, this can create a short term conflict, but the Gemini with their clever way with words can get Leo appreciating the advantages of any changes.

Leo are very determined and tend to stick to things that matter to them and see them out, they can find the Gemini's flitting from thing to thing annoying and pointless. Leo can help the Gemini to develop more perseverance.

A wonderful friendship based relationship that thrives in the early stages, but perhaps it will be a little trickier for you two to grow up around each other and take life seriously. Leo tend to hold back but the Gemini talkativeness manages to get things out of the Leo.

The Leo is the stabilising force and often the more conservative one in the relationship; the Gemini is the one who keeps up the pace and who initiates. Compromise is something you both have to work hard on, Leo are stubborn and this can be a big bugbear for Gemini.

Sexual chemistry is great: Leo's have warmth and passion and make ardent lovers while Gemini like to tease and can bring variety and spontaneity to the bedroom. Life is never dull in your bedroom and this is where you can work out many of your problems. The youthfulness inherent in this combination mean that your love life will stay active and fulfilling for much longer than most.

Gemini with Leo 1st Decan (born Jul 23 to Aug 4) – The relationship will have a fair degree of challenges but if you can face these head on you can build a strong bond over time.

Gemini with 2nd Decan Leo (5 Aug -14 Aug): This is the best match.

Gemini with 3rd Decan Leo (15 Aug -23 Aug): Combative and explosive as you are both headstrong and competitive, you could end up in a tedious and fruitless game of one-upmanship.

Famous Couples -Angelina Jolie (Gemini) and Bill Bob Thornton (Leo) are am example of this combination.

GEMINI and VIRGO

Mutable AIR and Mutable EARTH = Landslides.

Both these signs are ruled by Mercury, but that does not mean that things are all smooth sailing. You are both signs stimulated by mental activity, communication and learning; but while Gemini flits from things to thing like a bee bouncing from marigold to daisy to rose, Virgo are very focused, methodical and exacting with their attentions. Gemini are a little slapdash and Virgo are precise people interested in detail and perfectionism. It is this perfectionism and concentration on specific details that can drive Gemini up the wall. In a similar way, the Gemini way of skimming the surface and moving on is inexplicable to Virgo.

You both tend to analyse things and you enjoy debate and mentally stimulating conversations and so when you are chatting away things are going great, until Virgo start getting too into the detail. Details bore Gemini and so does routine and Virgo like their rituals and thrive on details. Gemini like to fly by the seat of their pants, but Virgo being an earth sign like some structure. Virgo are also restless and they love variety and yet they need to create routines and structure in their lives to give them security and they are highly specific about what they like and what they don't like. Virgo can be set in their ways and are not as adaptable as Gemini.

This is actually, despite what is said above one of the best combinations I have talked about; Gemini and Taurus works well, but there are less of this combination in real life. You will however find many Gemini with Virgo as it is exactly the earthy, practical and grounded qualities of Virgo that Gemini need to anchor them and give them more focus. The Gemini can help the Virgo to loosen up and smell the coffee and the Virgo can help the Gemini apply their valuable skills and mental agility in a more productive and focused way. This is thus a great combination for Gemini and Virgo who work together as well.

Virgo are organised both financially and domestically and can give Gemini that anchor and that stability which they crave. Virgo can help Gemini be more methodical and Gemini can help Virgo to take a broader and less narrow view of people and of life. Both these signs have a shy side and yet together they have far more confidence and can unleash themselves onto the world with a tornado of information and expertise.

Mentally, you have rapport and you interest each other; however Virgo are far more restrained and discerning about their contacts while Gemini are free and easy with everyone. Being with a Gemini can take a Virgo way out of their comfort zone; which is perhaps just what they need. The Virgo may help Gemini to have some more discretion. Gemini often play lose and fast with facts as they are more concerned with the overall picture, whereas Virgo are sticklers for accuracy and will pin Gemini down to get straight answers.

Gemini is a party animal and Virgo are work-a-holics; however when Gemini enjoy their work they are just as much work-a-holics as are Virgo and so this is an extremely hard working couple. Together these two can really get stuff done. Virgo is far more patient and is able to deal with obstacles and drawn out procedures more effectively, while Gemini can deal with people with great ease – this is where they can also complement each other. Virgo are consistent and can give Gemini that much needed safe haven to retreat to. Virgo are reliable, but they will get annoyed when the Gemini are late or careless about matters – Virgo are very precise, they do not care for those who are not punctual or not discreet.

Virgo are very honest; while Gemini often avoid difficult conversations. 3rd Decan Gemini are very honest too and so are a good match for Virgo. 2nd Decan Gemini like some sugar coating; they are more diplomatic and may find Virgo too direct. Virgo do take life more seriously and while the Gemini flippancy can concern them; I think that the combination of Gemini's more carefree approach with the Virgo seriousness can help Gemini to be more responsible and Virgo to hang loose a bit more.

Yes, there are things which annoy you both and Mercury ruled signs do get irritable and snappy, however there is so much you can gain from being together. You can enhance the intellectual capabilities of each other, foster success career-wise and have a wonderfully communicative, bubbly relationship. Fights tend to be over fast and while you do bicker and argue, you rarely fall out for days on end. You do need your own lives and cannot live in each other's pockets. Virgo like alone time and Gemini need their own friends, but it can work.

Gemini are jokers and they like to play pranks and tease; they must remember that Virgo do not like being teased and can be very sensitive to certain issues especially personal ones. Virgo take things to heart and take life seriously. Virgo are an insecure sign and Gemini need to learn where the boundaries are and to respect them early on. Virgo are very respectful and they expect that respect in return – take their individual needs and requests seriously. Gemini do help Virgo to see the funny side and not to take themselves too seriously – Gemini loves the way Virgo wit cuts right to the bone.

When this relationship lasts it is always because both parties want it to – these are not people who stay together for the sake of it

Both signs are nervy and can suffer nervous ailments and mental exhaustion; they challenge and stimulate each other and also stress each other out.

Virgo will reveal more and more about themselves the more comfortable they are in the relationship, however there is a problem: Virgo are more likely to want exclusivity and Virgo will want to be your king pin. Virgo may be threatened by the Gemini need to have a wide circle of contacts, socially and intellectually. It is not that Virgo are jealous, but they will hold back if they feel Gemini are not sufficiently committed.

Sexually Gemini are more playful and sensual; the Virgo is more conservative at first however once more comfortable in the relationship Virgo can be rather adventurous and very active lovers. Virgo pay attention to the details that can really make a sex life explode in terms of excitement. Virgo enjoy love making and there should be an active sex life that can sustain the relationship. The one problem for the sex life is both of your work-a-holic tendencies which can leave you exhausted.

The one downside to all the promise of this relationship is that you may eventually drift apart – this is a relationship where you need to make time for each other and to be alone together. You both battle to switch off and you both need to find ways of leaving problems and work at the bedroom door so that you can truly enjoy sexual bliss as a total escape which can really relax and rejuvenate. You both enjoy variety and so your sex life will not get boring and predictable.

Virgo add stability and predictability to the Gemini life and the Gemini give Virgo new horizons; they have great fun together and this pairing has great potential.

This pairing works well for same sex couples.

Gemini do well with 1st Decan Virgo born between 24 August and 2 Sept, although compromise and mutual respect is essential, as is finding ways to relax and knowing your limits – both of you.

Matches between Gemini and 3rd Decan Virgo born between Sept 13 and 22 can have a very loving and warm relationship with more affection and indeed great prospects financially.

2nd Decan Virgos born between Sept 3 and 12 can make excellent friends, confidantes and advisors for Gemini, although it may work better as a friendship as they may not see eye to eye on a daily basis especially if it is a 1st or 3rd Decan Gemini.

Famous Gemini-Virgo Couples: Elizabeth Hurley and Hugh Grant;

Courtney Cox Arquette and David Arquette; Helena Bonham Carter and Tim Burton

GEMINI and LIBRA

Mutable AIR and Cardinal AIR = Bright and Breezy

These two click right away and there is a good rapport and a strong friendship and sense of shared values. You are both people people and love to socialise and spend free time mixing and getting to know new people. Socially you are both expansive and very expressive, you enjoy meeting a wide range of people and learning from them. Intellectual challenge and stimulation is vital for you both and you will enjoy debating, analysing and teaching one another new things.

This is a very progressive, bouncy partnership and works especially well for couples from different backgrounds or same sex couples. Your friends will believe in this relationship and be supportive of you.

Libra as a cardinal sign can help to motivate and direct the talents and abilities of Gemini and the Gemini can help to energise the Libra with injections of new information and also help with development of skills.

Both these signs are mentally flexible and they can boost each other's mental capabilities by challenging each other with different views, the debate you share can enhance your reasoning powers and ability to solve problems and find solutions. This makes this a fabulous combination for business partners. Together you are an intellectual powerhouse and can make a big impact on society and how others think.

Libra will, in the main, be the leader in this relationship; the Libran will want to take the decisions and direct the financial and sexual side of the relationship. Libra have strong ideas of how things should be done and the Gemini should never underestimate the Libran. Sometimes the Gemini can feel dominated and side lined by the Libran and often the Libra underestimates the sensitive nature of

Gemini. Librans don't take orders, they often pretend to go along with what other's say however they are often doing their own thing.

The problem in this pairing is that the two of you may drift apart and there may be nothing to actually draw you back together. Passion is lacking here and so is emotional energy. Libra needs to be a better listener and be more understanding and Gemini needs to be more consistent and give the Libran clearer signals about what she/he wants. Libra can become annoyed by what the Scales see as fickleness and an inability to stick at things and Gemini can find the Libran way of life restrictive. Gemini are always 'ON' while Libra work in fits and starts, liking to be flat out interspersed with periods of total relaxation where they enjoy being very lazy. These two will not argue, when things go wrong they may talk it out obsessively but not actually get anywhere with the conversations – in the end they will pursue different interests and drift apart overnight not even knowing it is happening. Divorces between these two are usually rather amicable and can be worked out satisfactorily as neither hold grudges and both will want to move on.

In general, your lines of communication are always open and you will enjoy things together and then enjoy them all over again as you chat about them later. You can be best of pals stimulating each other's curiosity and need for mental challenge; you both like to be trendy to try the latest things and go to the hottest places, life is there to be enjoyed.

While starting a family will interest you both, you are not likely to not want to compromise in terms of your lifestyle and so starting a family is not something you should go for at a whim – you really need to think about how it could change your life in terms of time management and responsibility. If one partner (usually the woman) feels tied down and as if the other's life has not changed this can lead to resentment. You should however be able to talk about how you can both still have free time and how the baby sitting can be shared out so that the social side of life that matters so much to you both is not sacrificed.

The lack of emotional intensity with these two can mean the sex is a little 'wham bam thank you mam'; this is not an especially romantic combination and Gemini may feel they need to hear the words I LOVE YOU and feel the warmth in the embrace. The Libran however may not realise that the Gemini wants more and may go from year to year thinking the sex life is just fine. Sex is actually one of the things you both find hard to talk about. Gemini simply does not bring out the loving, tender and more affectionate side of Libra and while the sex has its fair share of excitement, it is never a full spiritual and emotional tornado that sucks you into another magical world. Sex is for fun, but it's not dramatic nor moving.

This is a pair who may both play away; neither sign are anal about commitment, they are both intellectual signs who are less likely to be bound by what the religions say about faithfulness and fidelity and more likely to see life as something to be lived to the full and for the moment. This will not necessarily destroy the relationship and forgiveness could mean you both carry on, taking a pragmatic approach. Jealousy is not the greatest problem, trust is and yet as you both verbalise your problems you can debate and discuss without conflict as neither of you like confrontation. Somehow the need in you both to avoid confrontation and the Libran need for harmony can mean that you are always keeping secrets from each other as that is just easier that arguing over the matters.

A wonderful combination for friendship, shared values and goals, mutual respect, intellectual rapport and fun. Libra helps the Gemini to initiate and be more pro-active in pursuit of goals, Libra can give Gemini oomph and self-confidence but cannot necessarily make the Gemini feel emotionally safe. Gemini can help Libra to be more flexible and more self-aware but a Gemini cannot truly fulfil the Librans need for affection and emotional warmth. While there is a massive amount of communication there is little understanding of each other on a deeper level and no catalyst to change or evolve.

Gemini match best with 1st Decan Librans (Sept 23 – Oct 3) – this is loving relationship likely to end up with marriage.

Gemini with 2nd Decan Libra (Oct 4 – Oct 13) – Sparks will fly as 2nd Librans are electric, excitable, open to change and anything new. They love progressive ideas and will enjoy vibrant, open minded Gemini; however although this is exciting and stimulating you may never actually settle down and the relationship could be very turbulent and unpredictable.

Gemini with 3rd Decan Libra (Oct 14 - 22) – There is an immediate attraction and things could become serious fast, the Gemini will feel grounded by the 3rd Decan Libra, the longer term picture could be more tricky with the Gemini feeling a little trapped and controlled.

Famous couples: Marilyn Monroe and Arthur Miller, Lindsay Buckingham and Stevie Nicks.

GEMINI and SCORPIO

Mutable AIR and FIXED Water = Storms on lake Eerie

A tricky combination that traditional astrology will warn against but which has some wonderful aspects which mean it can work. Somehow we gravitate towards challenges and it is via these very challenges often in the arena of relationships that we grow. This may be an odd couple combo and yet you have so much to teach each other.

While you may not be immediately attracted, circumstances may thrust you together and you may begin to be intrigued by each other. Gemini is a highly curious sign and the mysterious Scorpio is a baffling enigma which you want to get the measure of. Scorpio love the carefree, devil may care attitude of the Gemini and being with a Gemini can open up the Scorpio world and help the reclusive Scorpio to expand socially and shake off some of that reticence about meeting new people. The Scorpion is also an inquisitive creature and the Gemini with his wit and wisdom on tap is very entertaining and beguiling to the Scorpio. Gemini helps Scorpio to enjoy the lighter side of life and Scorpio helps The Twins to see the darker and often hidden side to situations.

Scorpio are very deep and Gemini are changeable and so both sense that no matter how long they know each other they can never really know each other and that makes both a little uneasy as both signs have to be able to figure others out. It can be a very cat and mouse relationship and there are many games to be played; both have a mask up and it can make for an uneasy yet manageable equilibrium.

The courtship can be like chess with you both acting coy even though you have decided you are set on taking things to the next level at least. Things can become very romantic but not in a conventional way.

Intense and fascinated by each other the relationship can move along nicely with great sex and more passion than a Gemini is used to. There can be explosive arguments and dramatic misunderstandings, but the Gemini will seek to smooth things over with understanding and the Scorpio will find it hard to stay angry with Gemini. There is something strong and secure about the Scorpion love even if it can be rather suffocating and restrictive at times; this is certainly a relationship where Gemini have to take the good with the bad. The Scorpio is a solid anchor, but their love has a price attached in terms of freedom. From the Scorpion point of view the Gemini may not seem a safe option as the Twin's personality is erratic and Gemini is hard to pin down. Scorpio hate fence sitting and are always very black and white while Gemini can be anywhere on the colour scale and are often on the fence. Gemini dislike conflict and Scorpio thrive on it. Eventually the drama of the Scorpion may feel like too much for the Gemini nerves and the Gemini may give up trying to understand the Scorpion. Longer term, as you can tell this relationship runs into trouble especially as the approaches of the two are so different. Gemini may find the Scorpion cynicism draining and the Scorpio at heart likes peace and solitude and will get worn out by the Gemini's constant need for social stimulation. Scorpio like to retreat and brood at times and their emotions can be illogical and even dark; Gemini seek to understand emotions with rationale and you can never really do that with Scorpio.

Gemini can bring more fun to a Scorpio's love life and the Scorpio can bring passion and fire to a Gemini both in the bedroom and in everyday life. Scorpio need intimacy and yet a Gemini illusiveness can prevent the level of intimacy desired developing and even if it does you may both quickly retreat from it and regret letting yourself go. You both know how to push each other's buttons and often your home life is like living besides a volcano. Scorpio like relationships to evolve and get every closer whereas the Gemini want a relationship that stays fun and which contains variety.

The sex is fascinating and a vital part of this combination. It can be like a chess game and sexual moves are rarely not premeditated.

Both can use sex as a tool of manipulation and there can be a great deal of mistrust sexually: the Gemini will always be competing with imaginary competitors and the Scorpio will secretly wonder how they measure up to the past lovers of Gemini. Both will tend towards adventure and novelty in the bedroom.

Gemini as symbolised by the Twins have a dual personality and Scorpio have as many layers as a large onion, which means this relationship has about 5 people at least in it and not all of them get along – sometimes it's magic and sometimes it's just sheer hell, the question is who will blink first and it is highly likely neither of you will want to walk away for some bizarre reason.

Scorpio have a need to settle down and they take family responsibilities very seriously; problems can arise when Gemini want to carry on as usual after the kids come along, still eager to socialise and maintain a youthful joie de vivre. This is especially a problem when the man is the Gemini. Gemini and Scorpio also have very different ideas on childrearing with the Gemini feeling the Scorpion parent is far too over protective and should allow the children more freedom.

These signs think very differently: Gemini are logical and analytical while Scorpio are incisive, penetrative, intuitive and cynical. Scorpio may think The Twins naïve and The Twins may find the Scorpion paranoid.

When the break-up comes it can be bitter and they are highly unlikely to remain friends.

This combination has the power to transform and educate you both – neither will ever be the same and you will not forget each other.

1st Decan Scorpio (23 Oct -2 Nov) While there is some mutual respect, you have vastly differing slants on life and it is very hard for you both to find enough common ground to get on. Gemini will be continually drawn into the Scorpio's issues.

2nd Decan Scorpio (3 Nov – 12 Nov) Can do very well with Gemini in a professional relationship. You may be introduced via networking or within your firm and together you can achieve a great deal over a long period with the Scorpio drive and determination and the Gemini people and communication skills.

3rd Decan Scorpio (13 Nov – 22 Dec) – Gemini may find 3rd Decan Scorpio too serious and the level of intensity will be overwhelming over a sustained period. The level of emotional commitment and demands from the Scorpio may be too much for Gemini and the Gemini may seem too flippant for the Scorpio.

Famous Gemini-Scorpio Couple: Baa Rafaeli and Leonardo DiCaprio

GEMINI and SAGITTARIUS

Mutable AIR + Mutable FIRE = Candle in the Wind.

A very good pairing and there are many successful relationships with this combination. There are enough differences to make this interesting and enough common purpose to make it work. You are both people with a zest for life, a love of change and a taste for adventure. You will spur each other on and life will be dynamic and never dull.

If you are teenagers both sets of parents will worry one of you is leading the other astray. Both of you enjoy the unpredictability of the other and this adds to the passion and fuels the fires of love.

Both of you need freedom and are very much driven by ideas and intellectual stimulation. Sagittarius is a risk loving sign who likes to fly by the seat of their pants, Gemini like to take you up on any challenge and go one better – the problem is there is little restraint and structure and you both can be like runaway trains. You may try everything and yet not achieve very much; it remains to be seen whether the Gemini will feel secure with the Sagittarian in the long run. There is no shortage of excitement with these two, but neither partner can anchor the other or give the relationship a foundation. When the going gets tough can you two pull together and knuckle down or will you both procrastinate until it's too late?

You do not always have a meeting of the minds and yet you enjoy discussions; the Sagittarian is an inspired thinker and the Gemini cannot always follow their logic. Sagittarians make leaps of faith and Gemini like proof and facts. Another problem in this relationship is the Sagittarian need to lecture and to give advice when it is not always wanted or even needed from the Gemini point of view. Sagittarians are often inspired by religion, philosophy or spirituality and the Gemini is more motivated by research and information that is readily verifiable. Exchanges between you are nearly always stimulating however, even if you do not see eye to eye. Sagittarius has a temper and yet is not one to argue, rather, Sag get angry say a few words then storm out – after which you will both probably go your own way for a few hours and cool off. Arguments are usually quickly forgotten and bridges rarely get burned – neither of you are vindictive nor spiteful.

The Sagittarian idealism can be inspiring for Gemini and the Sag may give the Gemini's life more direction and more meaning, Sag may help Gemini set long terms goals and work towards them. Gemini can help the Sag to think more carefully about details, logistics and technical issues and will help the Sag see the logical flaws in arguments. Neither of you are great with money and this is not a combination associated with saving! You both need to be savvier about household finances and rein yourselves in with the spending. You can both be spendthrift and throw caution to the wind when a whim strikes, however you like to spend on different things and while one may see a purchase as essential, the other may strongly disagree.

The Sagittarian may well wield influence over the Gemini and over time the Gemini may find themselves adopting the beliefs and morality of the Sagittarian. The Gemini must be careful not to go along with everything blindly or for the sake of being adaptable; the Sagittarian can sometimes be quite adept at pushing their views on others. Sagittarians are often religious and they may expect the Gemini to take on their religion once marriage takes place; the children will also have to be brought up in that religion.

Gemini are city people and Sagittarians love the country. While Gemini may enjoy city breaks filled with museums, culture and nightlife; the Sag will enjoy hiking, extreme sports and adventure holidays usually in the countryside. Some compromise is necessary. On the plus side you both love getting away and experiencing new places and cultures.

The Sag has a devil may care attitude and can often act recklessly and yet things still turn out OK; the Gemini at heart is a little more cautious and would like some more stability and predictability in life. Long term the Gemini need more grounding. The Sagittarian secretly longs for an anchor and someone to be more decisive, the Gemini indecision makes Sag insecure. Sagittarians value honesty very highly and Gemini although not dishonest can be evasive as that is their defence mechanism; this can make the Sag edgy.

This pair may break up and then get back together again constantly – they are impulsive and may have mood swings regarding each other. The relationship can start fast and will have many phases and fluctuations until perhaps you spontaneously get married – will it last though?

This relationship is exciting and there are many plus points and areas of mutual interest; your personalities are not dissimilar and yet the impulsiveness and restlessness inherent in you both can make commitment hard going. When one sign or the other is born on the 8th, 17th, 26th or maybe also the 2nd, 11th, 20th stability and some structure is added to the mix.

You can learn from each other and you can inspire and encourage each other; you can be the best of friends and if it all goes wrong you may still keep in touch and will never forget the great times you had. This relationship needs work and one of you will always have to grow up and be the adult which can lead to some resentment. It is a two way street and long term for this to work you need more restraint and more work from both sides. There are often unexpected hurdles with this pair and other people can prove obstacles to the relationship as well i.e. colleagues or family members,

It is common that this combination will contain people from different backgrounds, classes, ethnicity or culture.

In bed the fire of Sagittarius with the cheeky playfulness of Gemini makes for great sex, that is fulfilling for both. Your sex life will be very active and you are both usually up for it at the same time. Gemini make Sag passionate and you are able to gel well sexually, when you first meet you may not be able to keep your hands off one another. You both enjoy novelty and exploring new ways to make sex better; neither of you will get stuck in your ways sexually and long term things also look good from the bedroom point of view.

1st Decan Sagittarius (Nov22 – Dec1) – A very positive blend of energies mean martial affairs can proceed with success although Sag's wastefulness and obsessive need to go one better can drive the Gemini mad. 1st Decan Sag are never satisfied and can be adrenalin junkies who are always pushing the barriers.

2nd Decan Sagittarius (Dec 2 – Dec11) This is a less favourable combination for Gemini as the Gemini may find 2nd Decan Sag too bossy and domineering. This Sag is very opinionated and Gemini do not like it when they cannot get a word in edgeways.

3rd Decan Sagittarius – (Dec12 – Dec 21) This is the best combo of the bunch indicating good friendship and mutual support with a spark in terms of intellectual stimulation and the ability to work together.

Famous Gemini-Sagittarius Couples: Angelina Jolie and Brad Pitt, Marilyn Monroe and Joe DiMaggio, Isabella Rossellini and Martin Scorsese, Gena Rowlands and John Cassavetes

GEMINI and CAPRICORN

Mutable AIR and Cardinal Earth = A windy prairie in April.

This is the trickiest combination for Gemini and probably the rarest of all in practise. They are not immediately attracted to each other and yet long term there are some positives than can make it work.

This can be a frustrating combination for you both as you are so different and yet it is also fascinating as you can help expose each other to different worlds and different perspectives. The Gemini have a light and bouncy approach to new love and relationships while Capricorn enter all matters of the heart with care and deliberation. If it's got as far as dating then the Gemini should know the Goat is rather interested as Cap's don't waste time on people they do not see as having any potential. Gemini however will date at a whim and see how it goes and so the Cap should not read too much into the fact that the Gemini has agreed to go on a date. Gemini bring light hearted banter, fun and a sense of enjoyment to the relationship – the Twins can help expose the Capricorn to a wider social circle and can increase the confidence of the Goat, helping Cap to let his/her hair down. The Capricorn immediately makes the Gemini feel valued, respected and secure and that can be a very good feeling for Gemini. Gemini enjoy being with the firm and solid Capricorn and while at times Gemini can feel the goat is stuffy and conservative, Gemini enjoy it when the Cap takes control and acts decisively.

They both have a sense of humour – albeit a very different one, but both signs enjoy humour and like to laugh. Gemini will want the relationship to be very active and will be eager to introduce the Cap to new people, new activities and new trends – this relationship can be a real eye opener for the Capricorn. Caps are work a holics and while their work may get in the way of the relationship which is frustrating for Gemini, Gemini are pretty non-stop themselves and are also prone to never being away from their work in terms of email and various messaging. If these two work together they may never stop working, which can mean astronomical financial success.

Capricorn like commitment and will talk about that from the very start of the relationship – they like to know the relationship is going somewhere and trust is vital. Gemini are known to be commitment phoebes and while for the Gemini the fact that Capricorn want structure in the relationship is rather flattering and makes them feel strong and confident it can also make them feel as if they are being rail roaded. Gemini love to talk and yet Capricorns tend to hold things in and hold back – this can be a big barrier to them getting on and really frustrates the Gemini. Oddly enough, although Gemini talk about everything, they are less able to talk about feelings which is why they tend to analyse and explain them away, so here we have two signs who do not find it easy to talk about feelings and who in different ways deny their feelings. Getting needs met in the relationship is hard and understanding each other is even harder work.

Sexually Gemini can help loosen Capricorn up in the bedroom and the Gemini will be surprised by the ardent, earthy sexuality of the goat who once comfortable makes for an excellent lover. Caps are sensual, responsive, considerate and energetic lovers when they feel safe in the relationship, however if Cap start to lose trust and feel on shaky ground in the relationship, they can become brusque and mechanical. The Capricorn enjoys the variety Gemini offers sexually and will be happy to be exposed to new things over time. Gemini feel satisfied with Capricorn and feel safe.

While Capricorn may not understand the Gemini, they both have a sensitive side which they keep hidden and they respect that about each other. They have mutual respect for each other's feelings.

Gemini like space and Capricorn like solitude and that should be ideal as while Gemini pursue their many interests the Goat can either work or enjoy time out alone doing something they find fulfilling – in practise however this does not work at all as the Capricorn will wonder what the Gemini is up to and the Gemini may think the Cap is a stick in the mud or a wet blanket. It really is hard for these two to understand their differing needs.

Arguments will happen as the Cap has his/her feet firmly on the ground and may accuse the Twins or being flippant and irresponsible. The Gemini may find the Cap's need for structure and attention to detail demoralising and begin to resent their wings being clipped.

Over time the Gemini restlessness and the Capricorn need for control and routine can cause this relationship to falter. When one pulls away the other with tend to drift off and there may be little to draw them back together again.

When the Gemini and Capricorn ambitions are aligned this partnership can work very well as they have complimentary abilities and talents to bring to the table; however if the Gemini and Cap do not share a goal then the Cap need to work constantly will drive Gemini away. The Cap is prone to worry, they take responsibility seriously and may find the carefree, rather lackadaisical approach of the Gemini too much to handle. The Cap may accuse the Gemini of being irresponsible and the Gemini may accuse the Goat of being boring.

Cap are driven to succeed and they take life fairly seriously, but Gemini are driven to explore mentally and socially and these are very different needs that can come into conflict. The Cap can however help the Gemini to succeed by encouraging him/her to be more focused, strategic and determined, while the Gemini can help Cap network, charm and influence people. This is a good combo for political couples.

While this combo has challenges; human beings are attracted to challenges as it helps us evolve and often those relationships with more agro work better than those where everything goes swimmingly. In good relationships where there is harmony things can be taken for granted, but in a relationship like this where you have to work hard at it, you may get more out of it and in the long term you can grow together.

Gemini born on the 8th, 17th, 26th and also on the 6th, 15th, 24nd and 2nd can get on better with Capricorn than those on the 1st, 3rd, 5th, 10th, 12th, 14th, 19th, 21st, 23rd.

1st Decan Capricorn (Dec 22 – Jan 1) This is the toughest combo for Gemini to crack as these are Capricorns with a double dose of serious Saturn. The Goat may be too strong minded and set in their ways for Gemini. Gemini's whims will be too discombobulating for 1st Decan Cap.

2nd Decan Capricorn (Jan 2 – Jan 10) These two can harmonise and are likely to enjoy arts and culture together, this is a creative pairing with more affection and fun.

3rd Decan Capricorn (Jan 11 – Jan 19) – Far more mutual understanding and more flexibility from the Cap side make this the best of all three combinations for a successful partnership.

Famous Gemini-Capricorn Couples: Priscilla and Elvis Presley, Isabella Rossellini and David Lynch

GEMINI and AQUARIUS

Mutable Air and Fixed Air = High Pressure.

Two intellectual thinkers. This is one of the best combinations for Gemini. You will stimulate and excite each other and being together is natural and comfortable. You click from the get go and after a few dates may already realise that this is going somewhere.

There is lots of talk about and a mutual appreciation of interests. While you share many interests, you are just as willing to let the other one go off and pursue their interests and hobbies alone without jealousy or mistrust. You both enjoy freedom and yet here is a little secret, the Aquarian is a little more jealous than he/she lets on and just a tiny tad threatened by the Gemini independence. The Aquarian however plays it cool and he/she will not try and clip your wings Gemini.

The Aquarian is also sociable but in a different way to the Gemini who establishes an immediate rapport and likes to get on with everyone. The Aquarian has many acquaintances yet few true friends, the Gemini cannot tell the difference often between true friends and acquaintances and why should it matter. The Water Bearer has a little more reserve and can even been a tad aloof at times. The Aquarian is highly idealistic and the Gemini enjoys the ideas, knowledge and attitude of the Aquarian who is outspoken and often eccentric. They can talk all day and all night and they both thrive off the exchange of ideas; the Aquarian loves the way the Gemini knows a bit about everything and they both feel able to speak their minds in this relationship – not much gets held back.

While difficult relationships promote personal growth, this relationship although more easy going can also be vital for personal growth and development as the Aquarian can take the Gemini thinking to a new level and Gemini can wake the Aquarian up to what is under his nose. The Gemini can bring the Aquarian back down to earth as the water Bearer can be a little caught up in another world at times.

The Gemini changeability does not bother the Aquarian one jot, in fact he/she loves the way Gemini keeps him/her on his/her toes. The Aquarian is intrigued by the fun loving, carefree Gemini and finds the Gemini aura so sexy and very appealing. Aquarians can be worriers who take themselves quite seriously, but Gemini can make them laugh and can make them see the world from a whole new angle. Aquarians love the Gemini perspicacity.

The Aquarian mind is never predictable and while Aquarians are progressive and love to initiate change and espouse lofty ideals, they are often quite stubborn and set in their ways. This intransigence can surprise and baffle the Gemini who may find it a little annoying, however it is the very stubbornness about the Aquarian that makes the Gemini feel secure and safe. Aquarius being a fixed sign can give Gemini the anchor and stability Gemini so need.

The Aquarian values loyalty and likes a solid relationship, he/she is slow to express feelings even though he/she is quickly attracted to Gemini. The Gemini may not know for a while how much the Aquarian is in love, indeed the Aquarian may pretend it's just platonic when it jolly well isn't. Aquarians never forget their first love and if Gemini is their first love, this has got LASTING RELATIONSHIP all over it.

Aquarians have a strong sexual appetite and it will get stronger and stronger as you get closer and closer. Sexually, this is an exhilarating combination that will not get boring, however Gemini must always tread carefully as the Aquarian emotions are complex and deeply buried and if you ever act flippant about your love or unappreciative, the Aquarian could become cold and controlling.

The Water Bearer is not as changeable as the Gemini and once in a committed relationship the Aquarian may be less tolerant of the Gemini whims and impulsiveness. Arguments between you are not always constructive and may involve accusations and the blame game – you are better off giving each other space and talking about it later...much later. Not that you guys argue often anyway.

You admire each other and this can be a very creative partnership when you work together. You may not chose to have kids and you may well delay starting a family for a long while such is both your need for freedom and to have options open.

Both these signs need to be themselves and you are never judgemental about each other which promotes mutual self-esteem and strong bonds of love. This makes for a lively partnership full of cheer and surprises; you both like the fact that you embrace changes and are never quite sure what is next on the agenda.

It is never wise for the Gemini to pay a 'make him/her jealous' game as this can backfire badly. The Gemini is always one step ahead of the Aquarian and this is both vexing and very exciting for Aquarius, who hate anything dull and predictable.

1st Decan Aquarius (Jan 20 – Jan 31) Electric and passionate this relationship is exciting and dynamic. This is great for young love when you want to explore and experiment, the Aquarian may not want to settle down though and so marriage will have to be delayed indefinitely.

2nd Decan Aquarius (Feb 1 – Feb 9) Both ruled by Mercury you see much of yourself in this Decan of Aquarius who is more flexible, easy going and less structured. The relationship can be an open one and is great for progressive couples.

3rd Decan Aquarius (Feb 10 – Feb 18) The sensitivity, artistic nature and appreciation of arts and culture make this Aquarian and ideal match. The loving and kind side of 3rd Decan Aquarius helps soothe and relax you and there is an intense warmth and affection. This combo has the most romance.

Famous Gemini-Aquarius Couples: Heidi Klum and Seal, Dixie Carter and Hal Holbrook, Ida and William McKinley

GEMINI and PISCES

Mutable AIR and Mutable WATER = Drizzle

While this is a common combination and one that can work well it can also confuse the heck out of both of you. Your needs are very different and while you can laugh together and lose yourselves in another world dealing with the real world when it comes knocking can be a challenge.

You are fascinated by each other and maybe be immediately attracted. You share many interests and have adaptable natures. While you are both conflict avoiders who are easy going in the main, together however you can come into conflict. Both of you enjoy communication and yet while the Gemini is very verbal, the Piscean is subtle and can convey messages to you in a variety of ways which you may not pick up on. The Piscean moods are changeable and emotionally driven and the Gemini finds it hard to get to grip with where Pisces is coming from. Gemini get frustrated with what they cannot figure out and Pisces are not direct enough for Gemini. Pisces are dark horses, deep and mysterious with a highly intuitive way of dealing with life that jars with Gemini's need for analysis and pragmatism.

This is a very romantic combination and you can certainly enjoy the finer side of life as well as travelling together. Both of you love books and a good story or movie can really get you into a loving mood. Gemini will be the one who takes the lead in the relationship; Pisces go with the flow and are even worse at making fast decisions than Gemini. You both like to live and let live and make for a very likable sociable couple who will always have friends and family stopping by – your house is open house.

While this pairing can fall deeply and helplessly in love, making it work day to day can be fraught with problems. You are both erratic, changeable and restless and the Piscean can be moody to boot. The

Gemini is more contest emotionally and can find that the Piscean moods - which are hard for the Gemini to rationalise and deal with - set the Gemini off kilter emotionally as well. The Piscean does not provide the anchor the Gemini needs and the Gemini cannot provide the certainly and sense of direction that Pisces crave. You may drift along together as if bouncing on a choppy sea, going with the flow and not really achieving anything.

Pisces love with all their heart, they love unconditionally and do not seek an explanation for that love and so it is no use the Gemini trying to corner the Fish and asking The Fish for answers, definitions and analysis of the relationship. Pisces understand the Gemini better than any other sign and maybe better than Gemini him/herself and that can be disconcerting for Gemini as can the Piscean ability to predict things ahead of time and their uncanny sixth sense. Pisces have a natural ability to see beyond the obvious and that can help Gemini to understand things from a non-rational point of view, even if it takes time.

This pair can find it hard to work together and may have a very haphazard lifestyle, but this can actually work for them. They make wonderfully creative business partners and can come up with genius creations as long as they outsource all the finance and admin.

The Piscean can help teach the Gemini to relax which is very much what Gemini needs and it may be via this relationship that the Gemini gets more in touch with deeper inner needs and gains better self-understanding. At times the sarcasm from a wounded Piscean can hit the Gemini like a ton of bricks and arguments between these two can be bitter and hurtful. Pisces are slow to forgive and can hold onto things for a long while and so Gemini are advised to watch what they say or pay the price. At other times Gemini may feel dammed if they do and dammed if they don't; and this despair can permeate the relationship and spell its demise. Pisces should never underestimate the effect they have on Gemini; do not assume The Twins are carefree and untouchable.

This is certainly a combination which fosters spiritual growth for both parties as they have so much to learn from each other and the complications and often sacrifices of being together can lead them to stumble upon unique experiences to be treasured. Together you both can experience a special kind of magical love that enables you to escape and transcend barriers.

This is a very tolerant partnership and is ideal for modern couples and also same sex couples. It also suits couples living in cities in cosmopolitan fast changing environments. Children of this pairing will be brought up to express themselves creatively and verbally and will be highly open minded and socially adaptable. What these parents may not offer is enough stability and security, unless one of them are born on the 8th, 17th or 26th.

Sex in this relationship is vital for bonding and also communication. Pillow talk can be very productive and honest. Sex is also the way you escape from other hassles and bothers and where you lose yourselves to something greater. Sex is a great way of relaxing; never forget the power of foreplay and make time for sex. Pisces like to escape with sex and so no phones, no internet, no distractions and send the kids to granny.

1st Decan Pisces (Feb 19 – Feb28/29) These are the most idealistic and psychic of the Pisceans and if you are lucky enough to click this can be a otherworldly relationship where you are so in tune it amazes you both. 1st decan Pisces are physically very attractive and sexually gifted.

2nd Decan Pisces (March 1 – March 11) Very emotional and volatile it can be hard for the Gemini to deal with 2nd decan Pisces long term, Gemini may never know what to say such is the sensitivity and quickness to take offence. The Piscean demands emotional depth and needs a solid and caring force.

3rd Decan Pisces (March 12 – March 20) Love making is fabulous and frenetic and the intellectual competitiveness is fierce and fiery too. This Piscean can sweep Gemini off his/her feet. Thrilling, unpredictable and unstoppable. A magnetic combination.

This is an excellent match for Gemini born on the 7th, 16th and 25th.

Famous Gemini-Pisces Couple: Martha and George Washington

YOUR DAY

MAY 21

Ruled by Mercury and Jupiter

Lucky colours: yellow, lemon and sandy shades.
Lucky gems: yellow sapphire, citrine quartz and golden topaz.

(This is the day when the sun moves into Gemini. You are more likely to be Taurus if born East of London and/or in the morning)

Witty and playful, you have a youthful spirit and never stop looking to have fun and enjoy life. You enjoy news and current affairs and like to know what 'the buzz' is. Somehow you always know the hot gossip. You enjoy novelty; new things, new technology and new ideas.

You have an excellent memory.

Quick witted and good with words you enjoy debate. You are also nimble and good with your hands; you do well in sports of skill involving balls.

You do get bored quickly and you are very short on patience. You hate to be trapped in one place for too long and routine also gets on your wick. Travel is very much your bag, you also enjoy interaction with people of other cultures.

Your curiosity can be a negative trait if boredom or lack of mental stimulation drive you into experimentation which is destructive and irresponsible. Sometimes your seeking of new experiences and excitement leads you into misfortune or danger. Even the women on this day can be ladettes who love a fast car and sex, drugs and rock 'n roll lifestyle.

You make a good impression on people and should never take foregranted the lucky breaks that come your way. You are actually quite a hard person to satisfy. In love you may have numerous lovers and just never find the right one or maybe you are just too choosey.

Overindulgence, unwise spending and waste are two of your worst traits. You need to be more prudent and more considered when it comes to money.

With good manners, personality and a pleasing can-do attitude you create a good impression, so you are likely to be offered good positions in work and promotion – don't let your success go to your head. In your own business you will be able to find clients easily and being a work-a-holic you will do rather well. A bit of a party animal, once you get into a job you love you may actually neglect friends in favour of fulfilling orders/contracts.

Working in law, travel agency, IT consultancy, transport, logistics, trade, real estate or education are well suited to you. You are very effective as a freelancer.

You are a person of the world – older and very much wiser, you have a wealth of experience to teach and help others with. Victory against all obstacles in life is promised if you apply your wit and always extend your knowledge.

Significant relationships can happen in your 21st, 30th or 48th year.

A day of karmic reward, success which is often in later life is a test of your determination and wisdom gained.

Born on your birthday: Albert Durer, Robert Montgomery, Mark Cavendish, Leo Sayer, Henri Rousseau, Leon Schuster, Fats Waller, Peter Hurkos, Raymond Burr, Robert Montgomery, Nancy Travis, Mr T and Fairuza Balk.

On your day: 1984 "The Natural" a movie based on the book by Bernard Malamud, was registered.

MAY 22

Your ruling planets are Mercury and Uranus

Your lucky colours are electric blue, white and multi-colours.

Your lucky gems are Hessonite garnet and agate.

You are straight-talking, intelligent and use your foresight to make wise choices. You have high standards both in terms of personal integrity and in the way you carry out your work – you always have yourself under the microscope and expect a high standard of yourself and others. You are a progressive thinker and have a unique take on problems and creative approaches – you are not one to go along with what others think and will always form your own opinions. You enjoy learning and then passing that knowledge on to others; you are not one to keep your opinions or discoveries to yourself.

You are highly strung and have an abundance of nervous energy which can help you in responding and adapting to highly dynamic situations and taking advantage of opportunities on the spur of the moment, however prolonged periods of stress and tension can have a very detrimental effect – you are best off working in bursts and then having a cooling off period. You work well towards goals and are less suited to routine and monotonous work.

You are very excitable and bubbly and you need to find expression for this effervescent and spontaneous nature – when you are forced to supress this side of you, you can become depressed and demotivated.

You are excellent at making decisions under pressure and can use your powers of deduction and intuition to make excellent decisions on the spot. While your impulsive decisions often serve you well, you are warned not to throw away the hard work and effort you have put into something to make a rash point about something. Always take care in financial transactions especially where get rich quick schemes are involved. You hate wasting time and yet a certain impatience can grate against your more perfectionist nature – you need to find a balance between your need for speed and your need for perfection.

Even if you do make a bad hasty decision, you won't let that hold you back and you will not have regrets about it.

Those born on this day have their greatest successes when they use their mental skills and ability to think fast and make connections between things which others may miss; you can make money from being the first to grab an opportunity or see an opening. Mental strength, astuteness and willpower are your key attributes and can bring you great reward in your career and in handling other people with skill.

On the negative side you can be blinded by your ego at times and some on this date are very cunning.

Loyalty is a massive issue for you and you are rather suspicious of those you love and careful of who you trust, anyone who betrays you will be cast from your life. You are very insecure on the deepest level and very few will ever discover that about you; you have a very solid front which you project. You can be a task master and you love to be productive and achieving something all the time. You enjoy work and as long as you find an outlet for your mental abilities and energy and never forget to take regular rests, success is yours for the taking in life.

You have a wide range of interests from history to politics and tend to have a global perspective. Those born this day are often liberal and yet they never follow any crowd as such, as they make their own rules and live to the beat of a unique drum. They often revel in being perverse and shunning society and its values. Controversy excites them and they enjoy sparking debate and fuelling discussion, they like to play devil's advocate. They also enjoy espousing radical ideas. Humanity, liberty and fraternity is very much their motto.

Originality to their approach often brings them attention and fame and they make good inventors and social innovators.

A warning for those on this day is deception and delusion – you may often leave yourself vulnerable by not being able to see what is right in front of you. Although you are a good person with solid values you may don the old rose coloured specs thus not seeing the dangers and pitfalls within certain situations until too late. Always be careful of who you put your trust in, while you are in the main sceptical when you are chasing a dream you can be oddly blind to the obvious.

In your life you must uncover your own power to change things and to shape your destiny, you should never accept anything and should always strive to create change in your life and to grow as a person. The more you blend realism with your innate idealism and reject the obstacles put there by others the more you can succeed in life and find happiness. Learning who is good for you and who isn't is one of your biggest challenges. If you surround yourself with the right people you can be very happy and fulfilled.

Always be cautious about anyone born on the 8th, 16th, 26th of a month.

Born this day: Sir Arthur Conan Doyle, Novak Djokavic, Katie Price (Jordan), Richard Wagner, George Best, Morrissey and Laurence Olivier.

1819 The first bicycles called swift walkers were introduced to the United States in New York City.
1906 Orville and Wilbur Wright received a patent for a "Flying Machine" with a motor.

MAY 23

Ruling planet is Mercury

Your lucky colour is green.

Your lucky gems are Emerald, Jade and Aquamarine.

Those born on this day have kissed the Blarney Stone for sure; you love talking and communicating. You can think on your feet and are rarely lost for words, you are great at talking yourself out of situations and using your mind to find solutions to problems fast. Writing and putting thoughts into words is your forte.

Spunky, witty and fun to be around you can turn your hand to most things as you are versatile and creative. You are a people person who enjoys sharing and participating in things with others, you like to know what is happening and to be where it's at. If there is a party, you want to be organising it or being the heart and soul of it. You enjoy arts, music, current affairs and are an engaging conversationalist.

People enjoy your humour and your ability to joke, tease and make fun from every situation, however some may find you too flippant and unreliable. Humdrum routines and chores are an area of life you fall down on and accuracy and punctuality are not things you find that important – you are too busy living life and enjoying people to worry about the trivial. You enjoy starting new things, but your enthusiasm can often wane and you may leave it to others to finish what you started. You rarely persist at anything if it does not make you happy; you are good at getting out of situations which are in conflict with your nature.

You have the ability to see any life situation from a number of points of view and that enables you to form highly persuasive arguments and to reflect within you opinions a range of perspectives. You like to deal with what life throws at you in a very logical and proactive way – you are not defeatist but quick to think of creative solutions.

You are warm and friendly and while you can be a commitment phoebe, you always honour obligations and pay debts both financial and personal. You keep promises and always repay a good turn.

You have an adventurous spirit and are keen on gambling and taking chances in order to get a thrill or satisfy a curiosity. The sense of adventure often extends to science where those on this day can make amazing discoveries that can change the course of history. People born on this day are often revolutionaries.

As you are open to life, people and possibilities you are always attracting interesting experiences and little mental adventures. You will travel much in life both locally and internationally and meet people from diverse backgrounds. You enjoy learning and pick up titbits of fascinating information from every place you go and person you meet, this enriches you emotionally and mentally. You enjoy challenges and welcome debate and anything which is a puzzle or mental game.

Always on the go, you are not a person who settles easily – you must feel that you are in the mainstream of life and fully participating and involved in what is going on. You love to plan and are always thinking about what you want to do next, be it travel, a party, a hobby, a book or career-wise. Those on May 23 enjoy writing diaries, facebooking, scrapbooking and writing books.

Changing moods and erratic behaviour which confuses others can be your downfall and you need to seek more balance and establish more consistency in life. You get bored quickly and this can be the greatest hurdle in you achieving what you want to in life. You shy away from commitment and yet what you really need in life is more of a focus on commitment and structure, but no one is saying you need to be tied down.

While your first thirteen years of life are the most difficult often due to a hostile or domineering parent, once you reach the end of your teens you can really blossom as long as you are able to leave any negativity from your past and self-loathing behind - forgiving and forgetting is key.

You embrace change in relationships, social circles, residence, spirituality and political views; you are not stubborn nor intransigent and are happy to change stance in the light of new information. You may overanalyse people and relationships in a way which is often unproductive and which relegates emotion as a factor, favouring logic and facts. May 23's are often not in tune with their gut feel and they can ignore intuition and feelings; explaining them away. You need to embrace the esoteric side of life for a more holistic approach, rather than a head-centric focus.

An obsession with analysis and inconsequential detail can damage relationships as can the changeability and erratic nature of May 23. Love can be damaged by continual scrutiny and questioning WHY. Love defies logical analysis and must be enjoyed and experienced on an instinctual level; this is what you need to accept.

Those born on May 23 may well benefit from help from those in higher office, superiors or those in power. You are blessed with good luck and are humble in the way you attain success and acclaim. You have great inner strength and the power to overcome any misfortune.

Extremely resourceful and adaptable you are one of life's winners.

Famous People Born on this day: Joan Collins, Rosemary Clooney, Jewel, Margaret Fuller, Artie ShawMarvin Hagler, George Osbourne (UK Chancellor), Drew Carey.

MAY 24

Ruling Planets Mercury and Venus

Your lucky colours are white, rose, cream and pink.

Your lucky gems are diamond, white sapphire or quartz.

While finding your niche in life may not be easy, once you have you can achieve almost anything you set your mind to. Learning the virtue of patience is one of your biggest hurdles as is learning the true value in things rather than the superficial value.

You have a strong presence and are able to set clear boundaries which is a great help in business and personal relationships. You love to engage intellectually and socially with others and you have strident opinions which you are never shy of expressing, others find you authoritative and you command respect. You are very concerned about mutual respect and the acceptance of differences, but that does not mean you are not persuasive, you are always eager to win people over with your views.

You are gifted at sales, fashion and retailing as well as business negotiations.

When someone has finally won you over, you are devoted and a very considerate and loving partner. Your home is very important to you and you will want it to reflect your love of beauty and eye for detail. Your home will also be a centre for social and family events. You enjoy children and make an excellent parent who can nurture and be a friend.

You are very cheerful and have a pleasing warm and friendly approach, you dislike people who are rude and coarse and you enjoy refining your own manners and social graces. You are easy going and very accommodating, you are not one to throw your weight around. You have an eye for art, colour and are able to appreciate the finer things in life. You are very artistic and may gravitate to fine art, decorating, architecture or fashion. You are good at spotting talent in others and you are also able to see potential in things which others may miss. You enjoy culture and museums and make many trips away to expand your knowledge of cultural things.

You can often surprise others with your sense of humour and you may do well in comedy acting. Many authors, writers and teachers are born on this day as you love to spread your own appreciation of the arts to others and you enjoy the way one can convey ideas, concepts and messages via art forms.

Business ability is very strong for those born on this day and you have an excellent executive and managerial ability. You are good with money and can also make for an excellent accountant or financial administrator.

Your biggest challenge is identifying and clarifying an objective – once you have done this you are able to strategize and go for it. Often you can vacillate and be pulled in different directions making it hard for you to commit your energy to one path. With age and maturity comes success and the ability to know what you want. Your desire nature is extremely powerful and you can attract to yourself what you want for better or for worse so be careful of what you wish for.

You are a little like a cat who always lands on its feet; however this can lead to a complacency which is ultimately destructive.

You have very strong emotions and often ideas which are so set that you may dominate or control others without realising it; you need more balance in terms of your own emotions and you need to have more compassion and understanding when it comes to those you love. Learn that there is a difference between giving others what you want to give and what they really want.

While intensely jealous and moved to anger when the green eyed monster strikes, May 24's are generally pacifists. You can be materialistic and are motivated by money for the beautiful things which it can buy. You are often collectors or dealers in art or jewellery. You do not let go easily and are deeply hurt when relationships or friendships turn sour. You are skilled at negotiation and you do well in marriage counselling or where you can resolve disputes.

May 24's are highly effective combining a keen intellect, social skills and graces and artistic talent.

Famous people born this day: Bob Dylan, Queen Elizabeth 1, Priscilla Presley, Eric Cantana, Patti Labelle, Kristin Scott Thomas.

1982 Increased penalties for trafficking in counterfeit labels for certain works and criminal infringement of these works are added to the Copyright Act in 1982.

MAY 25

Ruling planets are Mercury and Neptune

Lucky colours are the darker green shades.

Lucky gems are turquoise, tiger's eye, cat's eye chrysoberyl.

Sociable and fun loving you amuse others with your wit and ability to tell stories, but your exterior conceals a serious side that not many know about. You never take anything at face value and you tend to look at situations and people with a deeper perspective. You have an immediate sense of people that is almost psychic. You are an extremely imaginative and creative person and have an active fantasy life which both relaxes and inspires you. You have a great memory and strong ability to visualise. You enjoy working with images interpreting art and literature and designing things.

You are capable of grasping concepts and ideas on both an intellectual, emotional and intuitive level and this gives those born on this day an ability to communicate via art or words that is both inspiring and exciting and which can have a great effect on others. You are able to instinctively perceive what others struggle to make sense of. You have a strong psychic and also a spiritual nature and your intuition is highly developed.

While your imaginative side can lead you to huge success it can be a drawback and a distraction if you are not able to find a practical outlet; developing discipline and learning techniques to hone your talents is vital. Sometimes you escape and avoid reality, your challenge is to master the practical and to be more determined and pro-active.

You must also learn to distinguish between those emotions and perceptions which are valuable and those which can be distracting and destructive. While your emotional intelligence is high, often you can read more into people and situations than is ultimately helpful.

Highly compassionate, you may combine your need to help others with your love of far flung places and may travel abroad to volunteer, raise awareness, educate or help with medical matters. Medicine and nursing are strongly indicated with this birthday.

You are an adventurer, but not necessarily a risk taker and your adventures are not always global but can be artistic and political.

You may often have prophetic dreams or sudden flashes of insight; you are a good judge of character. You may have lucid dreams or even experiences where you see ghosts or have other worldly experiences. Your dreams are extremely vivid and are often a form of escapism or even part of your job i.e. authors, film directors, photographers, script writers, poets and song writers. You may enjoy dream interpretation and find it useful. You tend to dream more than most and those dreams can have an effect on you and your decisions.

May 25's have a keen interest in anything esoteric: symbolism, mythology, space, religious mysticism, taboos, mysteries and conspiracies. Many of you have the gift i.e. are clairvoyant, clairaudient or psychic. You may be introvert and yet you exert a quite magnetism which is highly attractive and via which you can influence others almost unwittingly.

You work very well in psychiatric nursing, psychology, grief counselling, religious leadership and other careers where your calming influence and ability to deal with emotional people comes in useful.

While spiritual matters and the esoteric matter to you, you will always seek proof and will not accept anything with is vague and undefined. You learn from experience and your keen powers of observation. You have the rare ability to bounce back from disappointments and to truly learn from them. Your judgements are very accurate about people, but not always about financial matters.

The warning for those on this day is scandal especially connected to work; avoid gossip and backbiting and take care to always follow the rules within employer employee relationships as disputes can create great stress and financial loss.

Making money will never bring you as much peace of mind as using your creativity and intellect can. This is a day where genius can emerge if discipline can be achieved; avoid the dubious and stay away from alcohol, gambling and drugs. Impulsiveness and the desire to escape can be your downfall. Follow a clear path, pursue education either earlier or later in life as far as your possibly can and use your talents wisely and you will achieve fame and success.

Famous people born today: Robert Ludlum, Johnny Wilkinson, Mike Myers, Cillian Murphy, Anne Heche, Karen Valentine, Ian McKellan, Adam Gontier, Paul Weller and Dixie Carter.

1948 Andrew Moyer was granted a patent for a method of mass production of penicillin.

MAY 26

Ruling planets are Mercury and Saturn

Lucky colours are deep blue and black.

Lucky gems are blue sapphire, amethyst and lapis lazuli.

Your wisdom and insightfulness can help others to gain a better understanding of themselves and you can become an excellent teacher or mentor. Hard working and ambitious you hone your skills and work at your dreams with determination. You have a very organised mind and are able to structure your life to achieve great things despite obstacles. You know what you want and you go after it – being a Gemini what you want tends to change, but you will achieve many things of note throughout life in different areas.

You are diligent and methodical and will take your time over making decisions; you are less likely than other Gemini to jump into things, you like to assess and weigh up options and are not often rash.

You work very well in financially orientated jobs and have a sharp mind with numbers, data and when it comes to managing resources. You are conscientious and can work well where routine and focus are required. You are highly logical, have good concentration and strong powers of deductive reasoning. You are firm and command respect as you are able to see clearly what needs to be done and you have the strength to follow ideas through. There is a reason behind everything you do and you are rarely erratic and haphazard. You work well in business as with business the sky is the limit in terms of success and achievement.

Loneliness and isolation especially in early life are common on this day, but your best years are later in life when success and a strong sense of self emerge. You are slow to reveal feelings and slow to trust, but are extremely loyal to those you care for. Hard work is rewarded and your confidence grows and grows with age. You may well find you get on better with older people.

While you are highly gifted with intuition you may never fully develop it as you favour logic and careful reasoning. You take obligation very seriously and are a person who can be trusted and relied upon. Inertia and acceptance can be the biggest brakes on your development – you need to get the fire up within you to say ENOUGH, I AM GOING FOR WHAT I WANT. Never allow other people or perceived obligations to hold you back – it's your life too. Although getting going can be hard, once you are started on something you have the guts and determination to carry it through to a successful conclusion.

You are a worrier – you worry about achievement, your ability to look after loved ones and you worry about how to achieve happiness. You also worry much about disappointing others, you need to let up on the self-criticism and learn to develop peace of mind via relaxation.

People born on this day are full of contradictions; you may often find it easier to help others than to help yourself. You can be compassionate and selfless and have a great power to transform the lives of others. You must be very careful of whom you accept advice from and should always take advice with scepticism. You are best working alone rather than in partnership and in marriage you should always seek a pre-nup. You should err on the side of caution with money and seek to make solid investments rather than to speculate. Always proceed with caution with those born on the 4th, 13th, 22nd and 31st of the month – there may be a heavy karma attached to those relationships.

Most of the important lessons in your life will come via partnerships.

Famous people born with day: John Wayne, Lennie Kravitz, Sally Ride, Peter Cushing, Helena Bonham Carter, Peggy Lee, Miles Davis, Stevie Nicks, Matt Stone and Al Jolson.

MAY 27

Your ruling planets are Mercury and Mars.

Lucky colours are red, maroon and scarlet and autumn tones.

Lucky gems are red coral and garnet.

Curious, inquisitive, inventive and open to new things, your life will always be an adventure. You never stop initiating new projects and investigating. Friendly and helpful you enjoy engaging with others and are always open to learning new things. You make friends fast and you keep your friends as you are very giving and helpful. You are open to change, have a positive approach and that is why you succeed in life. You crave novelty, challenge and mental stimulation and get bored quickly. You are goal orientated and very motivated.

You are straightalking and folks can rely on you to tell them the truth. Sometimes your calling a spade a shovel can alienate some or cause opposition, but it is a valuable trait which can help you achieve things fast and establish boundaries. You have a critical mind and strong powers of perception. You have leadership ability and are highly organised and effective at getting things done or coordinating events. You may need to work on being more diplomatic and more moderate in your approach. No one can fault your enthusiasm but perhaps you need to learn to take other's opinions on board and be more inclusive.

You are good at appraising people and their abilities and your judgements are mostly correct although in some cases you could give folks more of a chance.

Those born this day make good journalists, critics and talk show hosts and may also excel in the courtroom or in business law thrashing out deals.

Versatile, restless and rebellious you will try many different things in the course of your life, you are unlikely to settle to one job for a lifetime and you are best off working for yourself and to your own rules. You are ever young and have a mind that always seeks new information and better answers. You are rarely satisfied and unlikely to settle for second best. You love travel and are very future orientated – you are always focused on what is next in terms of travel, career, where you live and what you can do.

You will pursue interests and seek to become an expert in the fields that inspire you; you may then wish to educate and inspire others with what you have learned. Your biggest challenge is focusing on projects through to the conclusion as often your enthusiasm runs out and transfers to something else. You are in a constant battle with your restlessness to establish solid bases and structure in your life.

Jealousy and suspicion can plague your relationships. Sudden changes in your attitude can make domestic relations tricky and you must try and be more consistent or perhaps you should take time to explain yourself better.

You have a keen intellect and can benefit from any education or skills training you can acquire – never miss an opportunity to learn. Living your life with zeal and enthusiasm is never a problem, but often to live it constructively is more of a challenge.

You are vital and enjoy being physically active. May 27's enjoy competition and are feisty when pursuing any goal. You like to be first and have a competitive nature. You like to tackle things head on and rarely shy from a challenge.

You will take on a dare although often you can be a little naive and can be cajoled into things which are detrimental. You often act then think and yet this impulsiveness opens doors for you as well as getting you in trouble.

You are quite vulnerable although you may look invincible. You inspire others and have great leadership ability. Although not stubborn, you will work hard to achieve anything you set your sights on and yet your goals can change over time, meaning you sometimes abandon one thing to jump on the next bandwagon. Sometimes May 27's lack the follow through as you get bored and want to move on to the next big thing. May 27's are better starters than finishers. You often make snap decisions, but you act on gut feel and instinct and this can often mean you make good choices without overthinking things.

May 27 is a very fortunate vibration which incorporates harmony, courage and power. You are naturally authoritative and have a commanding presence. Rewards will come from using your intellect and imagination in a constructive way. Have faith in your original ideas and follow your dreams.

Famous people born today: Henry Kissinger, Jamie Oliver, Vincent Price, Paul Gascoigne, Christopher Lee, Louis Gossett, Jr., Bruce Cockburn, Cilla Black, Allan Carr, Heston Blumenthal, Joseph Fiennes, Rebekah Brooks.

1796 James McLean was issued a patent for a piano.

MAY 28

Ruling planets are Mercury and the Sun.

Lucky colours are copper and gold.

Lucky gem is Ruby.

Determined, stubborn, persistent, dependant and with a strong will you set out to make your mark on this world. You have a great deal of common sense and are able to deal with life with humour and wit.

While you are imaginative and creative you are also highly practical and logical and can get right to the heart of any matter. You are driven to achieve recognition and are more likely to pursue life goals which allow you some limelight or give you authority.

You are driven by risk and valour – in some ways you live in a personal myth where you see yourself as a saviour or warrior. You have a strong sense of self and a feeling of destiny, you often live your life believing that everything will work out as you have a divine purpose. Curious about life and inspired to seek adventure, your life is constantly changing and you are always evolving in terms of your needs, goals and self-image. You like to discover new things and find ways of using that knowledge to inform, educate and lead. You lead by your thoughts and with your knowledge. You are an inventor and an entrepreneur.

You are an organised person who can strategize and actualise ideas. You are practical and need to be busy. You are energetic and have strong regenerative powers – you never allow things to get you down for long. You are very effective in business as you are not shy of making hard decisions and you have the courage of your convictions. You have a very practical side and can make judgements without emotional bias.

On the negative side you never tend to know when enough is enough and you must learn to switch off and relax.

May 28 often has a very strong attachment to identity and often identifies with nationality or religion very vehemently. Criticism is not welcomed because it is often deemed as a personal affront as you are invested in what you are and proud of what you are, that pride is sometimes too easily wounded. Having respect is important to you and you enjoy organising and taking control of people and situations.

You have an individualistic flair and like to be noticed; you are a trendsetter who revels in holding original views or living a life style which is unusual or inspirational. Although you have a lot of front, despite that bravado, you can be very vulnerable and tender hearted.

You are a good problem solver and leader as little gets you down; you are skilled at finding solutions and are rarely defeatist.

Strong viewpoints mean that you can be rather intransigent and inflexible in your thinking – sometimes you can express your opinions too emphatically. You can be very convincing, as you only say what you really believe and when you believe something it is rarely in half measures. You are not wishy washy, you are a definite character, with fixed ideas and motives.

You are a great talker but often need to choose your words more carefully, if you do they can have a tremendous effect. You are a good debater and will benefit from higher education. You drive a very hard bargain and are very astute with money – you fear not having enough money and that makes you cautious about spending.

Your health is good as you have a positive attitude and enjoy being physically active; you have good powers of recuperation. You enjoy the outdoors and love the sun. Work is very good for you and often the best thing for your mental health. Men and women on this day do well in large male dominated industries or organisations.

You like to look good and make an impression, you pay great attention to your appearance. Your emotional life is complex and you may attract manipulative or even dubious people into your life. You can be very emotionally intense in one to one relationships but are at ease with larger groups. You make a great travelling companion.

Although success is yours for the taking, caution is always advised with finances as your financial fortunes can go up as well as down. There can be losses in regard to misplaced trust in others, via legal battles and via strong opposition and undercutting from competitors. Number 28's sometimes have to start over again, life will certainly have distinct cycles.

Prudence and caution should always be exercised, but at the same time you should follow your passions with zest.

Famous people born this day: Kylie Minogue, Gladys Knight, Ian Fleming, Rudolph Giuliani, Kyle Brooks.

1742 The first indoor swimming pool opened in Goodman's Fields, London. Swimming as an organized activity goes back as far as 2500 B.C. in ancient Egypt.

1996 Theo and Wayne Hart received a patent for a ponytail hair clasp.

MAY 29

Ruling planets are Mercury and the Moon.

Lucky colours are cream and white and green.

Lucky gems are pearl or moonstone.

You have the gift of the gab and are never lost for words, you have a bright inventive mind and are full of ideas. You are magnetic and highly creative. You tend to ride on the waves of emotion and your life will have ups and downs especially in relationships as you are very idealistic and you go with you heart. You protect yourself with a tough outer shell and yet those who know you best know how vulnerable you are. You are stronger and more capable than you know and never take the easy way out.

You can be erratic and may find it hard to focus, but while that may be the case you are highly adaptable and able to spontaneously react to changes in the environment (beit business or relationship) and capitalize on opportunities. You are highly imaginative and capable of expressing your ideas with flair and impact. You tend to allow emotion to dominate you and so you need to surround yourself with positive people as negative situations can drag you into a vortex of depression and stagnation. You are a people pleaser and this can prove to be something which drags you off course. A big challenge for you is not to allow emotional ups and downs and passing distractions to set you off your course.

You are dogged by indecisiveness. Your creativity is the key to success in life and to the overcoming of limitations and obstacles. There can be a challenging karma to do with older women for those born May 29 and you may suffer emotionally at the hands of a mother, grandmother, older sister or female teacher. Extremely resilient you manage to build character from your disappointments and often your most rewarding career and life changes come later in life. May 29's make great public speakers, property developers, realtors or entertainers.

You can provide great leadership by expressing your ideas and inspiring others with them. An ideas person, you lead with heart and soul rather than pragmatism.

Sometimes talking or saying too much can be your downfall, avoid gossip and never rely on hearsay. You love discussion and the stimulation of people and debate. Always watch what you say as your words may come back to haunt you.

May 29's crave stability and enjoy a certain amount of predictability, even though you are somewhat restless by nature. You strive to build a protective wall about you and those you love and you seek an anchor in life; a constant which you can rely on. You are an imaginative dreamer who explores with your mind and who enjoys being creative even if you do not follow through on everything you start. May 29's fear the unknown and resist change especially in terms of emotional issues. Family ties and your home matters immensely to you. You crave owning your own home and will seldom rent. You are good with property and usually invest money wisely. Security concerns mean that May 29's are cautious and risk averse. You are a gentle soul and are not always strong and robust, although you have deep reserves of emotional power. May 29's need to look after themselves and respect their bodies.

Life for a May 29 should be seen as a journey where your moral or spiritual fibre is tested. Your goal is to learn to sort the wheat from the chaff in terms of friends, colleagues and lovers – many may disappoint you, but you should always learn and move on rather than resenting them. One of your other goals is to learn to deal with the uncertainty inherent in this day – you need to establish an unshakable inner strength and not to rely on material things and places for your security and stability. Faith in yourself and optimism are the greatest allies you have. Always take responsibility for your mistakes and forgive those who cross you, never seek revenge, seek freedom and good luck will come your way.

Famous people born this day: John F Kennedy, LaToya Jackson, Mel B, Bob Hope, Noel Gallagher, Annette Bening, Melissa Etheridge and Sarah Millican.

1826 Ebenezer Butterick the inventor of the tissue paper dress pattern was born.
1953 First episode of the "I Love Lucy" television series was registered.

MAY 30

Ruling planets are Mercury and Jupiter

Lucky colours are lemon, yellow and sandy shades.

Lucky gems are yellow sapphire, citrine quartz and golden topaz.

You enjoy the company of others and make for a curious and interesting companion. Friendly, warm and enthusiastic you excel in any social setting. While you have a wide circle of friends you are drawn to solid one to one partnerships and excel in this setting. You like to be in a relationship and also to have one Bestie you know you can rely on. You are a romantic and are very playful in love. You have a quirky sense of humour and are a lively person to be around. You love asking for advice even if you never take it – somehow hearing others' points of view gets the cogs of your own mind ticking. You also enjoy giving advice and are very good at helping others find both solutions and the motivation to deal with problems. You are very encouraging.

May 30 are very future orientated and you set yourself long term goals. You are eager to achieve in life in terms of education, places travelled and broadening your mind. You will strive to learn as much as you can in terms of both practical skills and also in terms of philosophical and social thought. You are able to see the big picture and are not a short-termist in terms of the actions you take. You are highly logical and yet often inspired by religion, belief or a philosophy.

You can excel in a career where sound judgment and fairness is a requirement. You are an inspiring person who can instil confidence in others, often others have more faith in you and your ability to lead and make good decisions than you do. You must trust in your inner voice and learn to take life one day at a time never biting off more than you can chew, as you tend to be impatient and craving of quick results. You are smart and quick-witted and have an answer for everything, you have a broad spectrum of knowledge and you know how to use it.

You have an uncanny knack of getting information and would make for a great detective or investigative journalist.

Not too much gets to you as you look at problems in a logical way and are rarely paranoid or grudge bearing. You tackle life with optimism and you are able to move on from setbacks quickly. Life for you is an adventure in which even the most negative events have meaning and value.

Your love of children and animals keeps your young and helps you to relax. May 30's have an ability to heal and excel in alternate medicine, traditional medicine and counselling.

One lesson you must learn is to cooperate more – you are very headstrong and independent and can sometimes appear defensive or uncooperative. You deal with your inner fears via faith and belief and you never allow those fears to take over.

May 30 people are driven by idealism and so whatever your course of action: positive or negative, misguided or heroic, you are driven by a deeply held vision of life. May 30's are seekers and are always looking for answers; superficial explanations will not suffice, you need to feel you fully understand, even when it comes to matters no one can ever as a human being comprehend.

You are a striver in all walks of life and you aim high in romance, career, social endeavours, sports and education. You are not easily deterred and will not let criticism or disapproval put you off anything your heart desires. You approach life with humour and energy and are fun to be with as you make everything seem possible. You hate liars and are good at unearthing deceptions – May 30's do not tolerate liars as you cannot see the need for lying, you are always truthful although somewhat blunt and direct for some tastes.

You can let your enthusiasm get the better of you and this can lead to exaggerations, overly highly expectations, a waste of resources and a scattering of energy. You often embellish, but you do not lie. You need freedom – whether it is freedom to roam or freedom of expression - and you will resist anyone who tries to contain either that freedom or your enthusiasm.

May 30's do well in academia as mental superiority is indicated. You can have great power in the mental realm of life and your words can have a profound influence on others. You may not seek material gain, in fact the material may be of little importance to you. You should never be intellectually arrogant and must always use thoughtful deduction mixed with the wisdom you acquire through your many travels. This is a day of journeys, a never ending process of discovery and re-evaluation of yourself. Writing is key to this day and whether you write fiction or non-fiction you will find the process cathartic. Often the loneliest periods of your life are the most productive and ultimately fulfilling.

As much as you enjoy people there is a side to you who is a loner; yes, you can back pack around the world by yourself quite happily just as you can spend long hours in the library or science lab researching and studying. You love to read and must have time alone to read all the many books you have on your list. As you grow older, quality not quantity is the way you like your social life. You love to spend time with nature and in the great outdoors with endless open spaces. You prefer the countryside to the hustle and bustle of the city. You love people and you also love your own company – yes, you can be confusing, but very unique.

Famous people born today: Steven Gerrard, Ceelo Green, Jennifer Ellison, Jane Seymour Queen of England, Wynonna Judd, Mel Blanc, Manny Ramirez.

1790 First Federal Copyright bill was enacted in 1790.
1821 James Boyd patented the rubber fire hose.

MAY 31

Ruling planets are Mercury and Uranus

Lucky colours are electric blue, electric white and multi-colours.

Lucky gems are Hessonite garnet and agate.

You have strength of character and the ability to use your mind in unique and original ways and this is what sets you apart. You command respect and are always noticed. Your opinions are often surprising and you tend to come at things from a different angle offering new perspectives; you enjoy debate and discussion and love to mingle with people from different backgrounds. Very determined, you achieve what you set out to despite obstacles and opposition. Despite being rather radical in many ways you are actually a person who respects and enjoys tradition – so you are a progressive conservative. You are expert in the art of conservation.

It is important for you to learn to prioritise and focus attention to make best use of your talents. You tend to scatter energy and give up on things too quickly in favour of the next big thing. You are filed with potential and yet fulfilling that great potential can be illusive. You are able to influence people as you speak with intelligence and can relate to people from many different viewpoints and perspectives. You are able to solve problems with your original ideas and you are able to understand complex problems and make sense of them. You are very independent and rebel against restrictions and controls. While you are inspiring you can be obstinate and you can sometimes get others' backs up – you need to work on being more diplomatic.

Your life is a search for answers to questions on which you put your own spin. You need to avoid prying into matters which are none of your business. You have a burning desire for an intense union with something with whom you share a deep intellectual and emotional bond. You believe in finding your soul mate, a person you are destined to be with. You have a freedom-closeness dilemma where while one part of you years for an all-consuming love affair, another part of you fears being trapped or restricted by relationships. You may find relationships are whirlwind and start and finish abruptly. You need a partner who shares your quest for knowledge and never wants to control you and stop you from being a free spirit. You do well working with your partner or in the same industry. Idealistic in love, you often put the person you love on a pedestal and set yourself up for a disappointment. You need to be more pragmatic in matters of heart.

You believe in the power of the mind to conceive of ideas which no matter how crazy, if they can be imagined they can be actioned. Improbability and uncertainly can never put off a May 31 who has belief in something. You often have the mind to go beyond science to make leaps which can seem bizarre, but which may create a breakthrough.

Impossible and NO are two words that call you to action and which you will rebel against. You are very much an intellectual type – you are a thinker and often a dreamer who enjoys using your ability to travel mentally to places unseen or unheard of.

While you embrace political, social and cultural change you are often rather stuck in your ways and can be stubborn about certain ideas you are attached to. May 31 often have habits and rituals which you stick to religiously; many of these habits are to do with personal hygiene about which you are fastidious. When you have made up your mind about something you will not take kindly to be persuaded otherwise – there is method in your madness and while others may not understand, you know it makes sense in your world.

You are a self-contained, self-sufficient person and will often experience loneliness in your search for people who get you and for that soul mate. Loneliness is often the price you pay for your freedom. May 31 often exhibit genius, they can however be ahead of their time and misunderstood. You may shun material things for enjoyment of nature and study.

Famous people born this day: Clint Eastwood, Brooke Shields, Colin Farrel, Phil Keoghan, Tom Berenger. Casey James.

1892 Lea & Perrins Worchestershire Sauce became a registered trademark.

JUNE 1

Ruling planets are Mercury and the Sun.

Your lucky colours are copper and gold.

Your lucky gem is Ruby.

Artistic and original you take the world by storm and stand out from the crowd. Your thoughtfulness and interest in other endears you to people. You are witty and vibrant. Sometimes moody and seemingly confused and at other times highly practical and driven, you are never to be underestimated. You are idealistic and inspired in the way you live your life, you are often carried along on a wave of enthusiasm. You tend to follow your head rather than your heart and yet it is your head that gets you into more trouble while learning to trust your intuition could be the best thing for you.

You have a great deal of charisma and you pay attention to your looks and attire, wanting to create a good impression – you dress to impress and have a style of your own. You are a born leader who can use your influence for good or bad – you will gain positions of leadership without even aiming for them and the challenge is for you to use those opportunities for positive purposes. People look up to you and in any walk of life you can gain respect and take control.

While you enjoy being around people, you often are less interested in others than you are in yourself, you like to hold the floor and can often be impatient. You are highly capable intellectually and love new ideas and the way one can open doors via new inventions. You are an early adopter and relish opportunities to try new things and cutting edge technology. While making money matters to you it is your intellectual and communicative achievements that fulfil you the most.

June 1's enjoy the limelight and are often performers – they may well have a shy side and yet externally they are gregarious and outgoing. You can be flamboyant and enjoy being known for your style and pazzaz. You usually know when a June 1 walks into the room as you radiate energy and take the room by storm. Although you can be a very private person, you know how to manage a very public façade.

Strong viewpoints mean that the June 1 person can be rather intransigent and inflexible in their thinking – sometimes they can express their opinions too emphatically. You can be very convincing, as you only say what you really believe and when you believe something it is rarely in half measures. You are not wishy washy, you are a definite character, with fixed ideas and motives.

You are stubborn and yet that stubborn determination helps you to endure hardship and long spells of disappointment without losing sight of your goals. You seek autonomy and must have authority in some aspect of your life or you can feel highly frustrated. Constantly playing second fiddle offends your ambitious nature and can bruise your ego; as cream rises to the top, June 1's must rise to #1 spot in some respect of your lives. You like to make your mark and if you are not noticed in a positive way you may become controversial to stir up attention, it is of course always preferable for you to be respected.

You like to help others and protect the vulnerable, however sometimes you enjoy the power which being a saviour gives you over the saved and you can offer your assistance in exchange for a tacit bond of control. You need to learn to give with no strings attached, emotional or otherwise. You enjoy giving advice even if it is not asked for, you are very opinionated on most matters.

You benefit from hard work and the more you struggle to achieve something the more you value that achievement. Often your greatest weaknesses become your greatest strengths and the spiritual growth from this transformation is very beneficial for you. If you are a June 1 and you become a defeatist quitter you will live a life of drudgery and boredom.

Often those on this day have fluctuating health – you will be inclined to change doctors and try many different alternative and traditional medical methods to find solutions. Like everything in your life, your troubles with health can lead you to a healthier way of living which means that in the long run you are more healthy than most. Prevention is better than cure and natural methods work well for you – always get a second opinion or even a third on medical matters.

While you may take a while to make a decision, once you have decided on a course of action you put the force of your will behind it and there is no stopping you.

Famous people born on this day: Marylin Monroe, Morgan Freedman, Heidi Klum, Alanis Morissette, Pat Boone, Ronnie Wood, Andy Griffith and Jason Donovan.

1869 Thomas Edison obtained a patent for an electrographic vote recorder.

JUNE 2

Ruling planets are Mercury and Moon

Lucky colours are cream, white and green.

Lucky gems are moonstone or pearl.

A great friend and companion who comes into their own in close one to one relationships, you are loving, thoughtful, warm hearted and kind. You are very enterprising and can accomplish great things in business, but anything you do needs to be from the security of a solid base. Family, stability and security matter to you and you may well marry early in life as you are not a person who likes to be alone. Many June 2's stay at home with the family for a long period as they enjoy the homely environment. You will set out to establish yourself in the world by getting a good education or a getting a solid job, securing yourself a home and setting money aside – once this is achieved you will become more adventurous. You have great business and financial acumen.

You are a very reliable person who offers consistency in love and friendship; however you can often be controlling with those you love in order to maintain that stability you crave. You are a stubborn person and when you dig your heels in you are immovable. You need peace and harmony and are often cast in the role of peacemaker – you are not confrontational and in the main are diplomatic. You have good persuasive skills and can win people around with your humour and common sense.

It is important to you to be liked and to be popular in your social circle, you enjoy being with people and you have strong feelings about who you like and dislike. Your emotions are never far from the surface and you can be a little moody at times. You are very ambitious and do not like waiting for things to come your way. Very artistic and imaginative you have an eye for colour and form and can make a great designer or architect.

You go for what you want, but what you want can fluctuate and you often struggle in early life to find what really fulfils you – you may go after things with passion only to find that the grass was not greener and then you are on to the next thing which you hope will offer mental and emotional fulfilment. Your life path is one of many routes chosen and many routes followed – variety is the key and change is essential.

You are a quick and intuitive thinker with a feel for markets, sales and other people; you are a good judge of mood and emotion and when to make a move. You work very hard, but can be hard to work with. You are a very direct and honest person.

June 2's can do very well with property, real estate and mining/mineral investments. You have a flair for the arts and can also excel in industries where cutting edge technology is key.

While you occasionally gamble in business, you like rock solid security in love and only invest in long term meaningful relationships, you have no time for flings and one night stands. Mental rapport and emotional understanding are both key to you in relationships.

Your forthright charm, straightforward demeanour and wit get you where you want to go.

You have a psychic ability and are very tuned in to the emotional atmosphere at any moment; you have good timing due to your ability to suss out people and anticipate trends. You are gifted in business due to a knack with money and good intuition. Romantic in terms of emotional attachment and also in your view of life, you can be very sentimental and tend to hoard items ie photographs, mementoes, items passed down in the family etc. to which you often attach emotions. Things matter to you – you will accumulate a great number of possessions throughout life and it is not the monetary value, but the sentimental value of these which matters.

You can become gloomy and depressed due to an obsession with loss which becomes more intense in times of crisis and change. You tend to fear the loss of anything from friends, family, property money, love, a job, a teddy bear etc. June 2's have a problem letting go; they fear death in terms of the dissolution of the body and the obscurity it represents – these fears can give rise to a controlling nature and a tendency towards anxiety and worry. You need to control things to prevent separation and to hold on to what you have.

You have a flair for business and are highly practical and astute with financial affairs and money management.

June 2 do not leave things to chance, they like firm arrangements and to have a clear plan – you prefer your life to be organised. June 2 are often fanatically devoted to the parents especially the mother.

You make an excellent parent and enjoy family life, although you can be over protective and even a hypochondriac in your hysteria about the health of loved ones. You are very good with food and are in general concerned with health and well-being. You have a drive to care for others and can fuss about even when it is not needed.

Famous people born on this day: Thomas Hardy, Jerry Mathers, Dana Carvey, Bo Diddley, Tony Hadley, Sergio Aguero, Justin Long and Willy Moon.

1906 "Your a Grand Old Flag" by George M. Cohan was trademark registered.
1857 James Gibbs patented the first chain-stitch single-thread sewing.

JUNE 3

Ruling planets are Mercury and Jupiter.

Lucky colours are yellow, lemon and sandy shades.

Lucky gems are yellow sapphire, citrine quartz and golden topaz.

You are an excellent raconteur and speak with zest and enthusiasm. You are popular because of your optimistic and happy vibe – you make others around you feel good. You are perceptive and imaginative and with a strong will can make some great achievements and progress in life. People often underestimate you as you do not come across as ambitious, but you are very goal orientated.

You may struggle with learning when you are young due to a rebellious streak and an inability to concentrate, but your sense of adventure and irrepressible spirit will serve you well later in life. You never take no for an answer and you do not allow opposition to get you down – you think rules are made to be re-made. With maturity, you become a force to be reckoned with intellectually and in terms of your ideas.

You are a person who thinks big and has a can do attitude, but you must be careful of not biting off more than you can chew.

You have high standards morally and ethically and adhere to the principles of fairness and integrity in all walks of life. You are generous to those less fortunate and like to give folks a helping hand when and where you can. You are a lucky person who always lands on your feet, but you are always aware of those less fortunate. You are a great manager and good at making forward thinking plans which are inclusive and which are beneficial to wider society. You care about the planet and people beyond your immediate circle and you want your life choices to reflect your compassion, concern and empathy for others. You are not a short term thinker for short term gain, you see a bigger picture and a longer term solution.

Politics may attract you as you are socially and community orientated and like to make a difference. You have an honest, well balanced persona and your judgement and advice are good – you make a wise friend and confidant.

Jovial and often a prankster who loves to laugh, you are number one on the guest list for parties. You are quite exuberant and yet sometimes you need to contain your enthusiasm and let other more shy and retiring types get their voices heard. You are good at organising and getting things done. People admire the way you bounce back and never let things get you down; your upbeat and zealous nature ensures life is never boring. Learning to relax and let your batteries recharge is a lesson you will not learn easily.

The mysteries of life are contained within the changes you will go through. June 3's are interested in meaning and you may find that via religion, faith or science. The endings and beginnings in your own life will have much to tell you about yourself, your karma and life's meaning. Remember that not everything can be achieved through hard work; sometimes you must sit back and wait for a wave which can carry you back to shore. Look beyond the material to see the spiritual cycle behind events and what that can teach you. Yours is a life of change and a personal adventure to be lived, but always with a spiritual awareness. Discipline and vision are the key ingredients to keep despair at bay and inspiration in your heart. You can; in dealing with your own problems and crises become a beacon of hope to others going through similar things.

June 3's can let their enthusiasm get the better of them and this can lead to exaggerations, overly highly expectations, a waste of resources and a scattering of energy. You often embellish, but you do not lie. June 3's need freedom – whether it is freedom to roam or freedom of expression - and you will resist anyone who tries to contain either that freedom or your enthusiasm.

June 3's often travel the world, feeling more at home in foreign lands than you do at home – you love to absorb other cultures and learn as much as possible about the religions, ethnicities and geography of far flung places. You love the outdoors and wise open spaces and are an adventurer who relishes finding new frontiers i.e. space, Antarctica, science, the ocean.

Blood is thicker than water is NOT the motto of June 3 and you may often lose touch with family in favour of friends who share your passions and goals. June 3 like to move on and are not always good at keeping in touch – new day, new people, new places and you do not always look back. You must have freedom in relationships and will not value commitment above all else – June 3 often enjoy unconventional or open relationships and will have many partners throughout their life.

June 3's love being active and so physical activity and sports are always a big part of your life; you are competitive. There is a love for animals as well as wildlife and a June 3 may devote their life to protecting animals (mammals or sea-life) in terms of conservation. June 3's value the environment, you may live in a town, but you love to get away to the country and be at one with nature. You would prefer to live in the countryside.

With age, June 3's become wise philosophers who rarely grow old and bitter – in fact you will always retain a youthful spirit. You will always be a dreamer working on some goal. Many June 3's who cannot study further at a young age, achieve in academia later in life.

Famous people born this day: Rafael Nadal, Anderson Cooper, Imogen Poots, Tony Curtis, James Purefoy, Suzi Quatro, Wasim Akram, Papiss Cicce, Jill Biden, George V, Allen Ginsberg, Josephine Baker, Lili St. Cyr, Chuck Barris and Raul Castro.

1969 New York Rangers was trademark registered.
1934 Dr Frederick Banting the co-inventor of insulin was knighted.

JUNE 4

Ruling planets are Mercury and Uranus

Lucky colours are electric blue, white and multi-colors.

Lucky gems are hessonite, garnet and agate.

You have a good head on your shoulders and can get things done especially in business that relates to emerging fields, alternate fields or science. Very much with a mind of your own, you often say what no one else dare say, truth and social justice mater to you and you will rebel against the established order in whatever field you find yourself in.

June 4 is about being radical, original, inventive, ahead of your time, individual and controversial. June 4's think they are very tolerant, but they are more tolerant of what is 'out there' and often not as tolerant towards tradition, conservative views and the establishment. This day is associated with genius, fame and turbulent times.

You are often misunderstood as your ideas are ahead of their time and you are an enigma especially to those who are security conscious or dominated by their emotions and immediate concerns. You have a wide range of interests from history to politics and tend to have a global perspective. June 4's are often liberal and yet they never follow any crowd as such, as they make their own rules and live to the beat of a unique drum. You often revel in being perverse and shunning society and its values. Controversy excites you and you enjoy sparking debate and fuelling discussion, you like to play devil's advocate. You also enjoy espousing radical ideas. Humanity, liberty and fraternity is very much your motto. Originality to your approach often brings you attention and fame and you make for a good inventor and social innovator.

Hard working and conscientious, you do your best work when inspired or driven by a cause. When you have the bit between your teeth you know no boundaries and can sometimes push yourself and others too far. While you are compassionate and opinionated you may come across as bossy or arrogant and you need to work more on being diplomatic – having said that your unusual way of communicating can grab attention and make a difference.

Highly original, you will pursue the path less trodden in life and excel in fields where thinking out the box and being a bit out there matters. You do not fare well in regimented and conservative traditional careers. You resist control and restriction and must have freedom to think and act. Relations with your parents can be volatile.

While you are very methodical and analytical you need to temper your opinions and make space in your life for the opinions of others. Often when you have a bee in your bonnet you become blind to other options which may be just as valid or laudable. You are a perfectionist and can often drive yourself mad with self-criticism, you need to develop more self-worth, as while you are confident, you may lack self-love and self-understanding. You need to learn to relax as you may end up suffering from burnout.

This day is one of extremes and often extreme wealth or fame can be a burden. Often there can be a neglect of spiritual life for worldly achievement and success or perhaps spiritual goals get somehow mixed up with material ones and meaning is lost. Your ego must be managed and your true emotional drivers acknowledged – learning to know yourself and understand yourself is a challenge.

June 4 are not scared of being unpopular if they believe in what they are doing and that can make them extremely powerful and effective. June 4 are the people you get in when you have run out of ideas and need help out of a mess; they can sort things out. You aim to be true to yourself rather than popular and are not a people pleaser. A June 4 will stick their neck out. You have a keen sense of what needs to be done and while others may not like it, you are most probably right.

June 4' are often attracted to the sciences and technology worlds.

You may actually come across as cold or hard – it may be that you find it easier to be compassionate to groups than individuals. The truth is you are not cold, you are a great philanthropist with wisdom and the power to work for good. You are born to wield power and create progressive change. Negatively, some on June 4 pursue money and power obsessively and insatiably, taking a hard boiled approach to business and life.

When you take a gamble you seldom lose. Women with this placement should never get emotionally involved in business and should not allow personal frustrations to impair their professional judgment. Men and women on this day are very positive and proactive.

You are destined to be a top dog and you will make money or find backers to help you achieve what you desire.

Famous people born this day: Angelina Jolie, Russell Brand, Lukas Podolski, George III, Bradley Walsh, Evan Spiegel, El Debarge, Luisa Zissman, Dr. Ruth Westheimer, Parker Stevenson, Bruce Dern.

1963 Patent #3,091,888 was granted to six-year-old Robert Patch for a toy truck.

JUNE 5

Ruling planet is Mercury.

Lucky colour is green.

Lucky gems are Emerald, Aquamarine or Jade.

Variety is the spice of your life and you need to have many things on the go at once to feel alive. You get bored quickly and like to fly by the seat of your pants and respond to impulses. You hate routine and structure.

You are suited to creative jobs and careers where communication is key. You also enjoy careers where travel is a constant and you may well drive or travel for a living. Financially you need to learn discipline and prudence: you must plan and manage your money well. You are an ideas person however you are not very good at managing people or resources. You are best placed communicating, teaching and generating creative ideas – then you should leave the finer details and organisation to others.

You are very curious and observant and you just cannot get enough information; you have wide ranging interests and pursuits. You make for an excellent journalist as you enjoy uncovering facts and putting your interpretation on them. You are addicted to devices ie phones and tablets and can find it impossible to switch off mentally.

You enjoy being among people and are not a loner. The world is a place filled with interest and opportunities to learn and meet new people, you are less concerned with destiny, fate and spiritual matters.

You are fun to be with as you are lively, chatty and interesting; you are highly adaptable and non-judgmental and people love that about you. You often confuse your partner or lover as you are very changeable and you can be very indecisive, but life around you is never dull. You will have many significant relationships in life and you never stay where you are unhappy. You live for the moment and you make each moment count. You are not one to worry about tomorrow – tomorrow is just another day to enjoy.

You are an inventive person capable of quickly finding solutions or talking yourself out of problems, you are skilled verbally and can get a message across. You have a non-threatening manner which makes you easy to be around and you are neither bossy nor oppressive. You enjoy jokes and like to see the funny side of life. You like to find ways of doing everything fast and are a highly efficient person. Your worst problem is distractions – you often lose focus before finishing a project. When something interests you, you can be extremely productive. You are very good at working with your hands and can pick up skills and also languages fast. You may well be good at sports where agility is required. You have an excellent ability to absorb and remember information.

You may not be competitive or ambitious – for you, life is about having fun and doing and seeing as much as possible. Learning to relax and slow down a little is a challenge for you.

You are a bundle of nervous energy and are quite excitable; do not burn the candle at both ends, learn to relax and calm yourself down. Eat loads of fresh foods rich in Vitamin B's.

You adore children and are excellent at working with and teaching them. You have good relations with your siblings and enjoy family activities. You will want to have a family of your own and will be a friend to your kids. June 5 people are ever young and you never get old and cynical. June 5 people relate well to all age groups and social groups.

You have an ability to know the value of something when you see it and that can make you skilled at retail and as a collector. When you make money you will give generously as you have a philanthropic bent.

Your life is one of change and unpredictable events which can often shock you. While sometimes there are struggles to be overcome you can always rely on your network of friends and ability to enjoy the little pleasures to get you though. Your biggest asset is your mind and your power to adapt to changes and make the very best of them. You have a strong character and are determined. You are coloured and shaped by your early life and often the difficulties or attitudes you learn as a child are hard to shake off and may cause you to make mistakes later on in life. You can also be drawn into trouble by going with the crowd and following first and thinking second. In your work you are diligent and dependable and you enjoy receiving praise.

Women on June 5 can be of invaluable help in their partner's business. Often the men on this day are overprotective and can be prone to tantrums born of frustration. You are more sensitive than you look and others often underestimate your tender hearted side.

June 5's crave the stimulation of travel and new people and places. Your life is full of short journeys and longer ones whenever possible. You change residence often and may rent rather than buy for the freedom that offers. When a 5 June outgrows something they move on – no regrets, they take everything life throws at them as an experience to learn from.

June 5 embrace change in relationships, social circles, residence, spirituality and political views; you are not stubborn nor intransigent and are happy to change stance in the light of new information. You can overanalyse people and relationships in a way which is often unproductive and which relegates emotion as a factor, favouring logic and facts. You are often not in tune with your gut feel and you can ignore intuition and feelings; explaining them away. You need to embrace the esoteric side of life for a more holistic approach, rather than a head-centric focus.

An obsession with analysis and inconsequential detail can damage relationships as can the changeability and erratic nature of the June 5. Love can be damaged by continual scrutiny and questioning WHY. Love defies logical analysis and must be enjoyed and experienced on an instinctual level; this is what you need to accept. You need to be more secure in relationships and react less to small matters. Less talk, more affection and more body language can do relationships good. Love is not logical.

June 5's can find it hard to know themselves and they confuse the heck out of others. While you seek to dissect everything and critically evaluate it, you also like to chase ideals at times, in contrast to your usual demand for hard evidence, which goes out the window if something inspires you.

June 5 live on their nerves and crave excitement but living such a hectic life can take its toll and you may suffer from mental health issues and stress later in life.

June 5's do well in life as they are flexible and adaptable and tend to bounce back from most things.

Famous people born this day: Kenny G, Adam Smith, Robert Kraft, Jade Goody, Pancho Villa, Bill Moyers, Robert Lansing.

1984 Safety Cap for a Medicine Bottle patented by Ronald Kay.

JUNE 6

Ruling planets Mercury and Venus.

Lucky colours are white, cream, rose and pink.

Lucky gems are diamond, white sapphire or quartz crystal.

Charming, engaging and a pleasure to be around, you find it easy to establish a rapport with most people. While you are diplomatic and friendly you can fall foul of judging books by the covers and you may wish to surround yourself with beautiful places and people shielding yourself from the coarser side of life. "Manners maketh man," is your motto and you are proud of being a person who avoids conflict and who acts as peacemaker. You will be civil even towards your enemies. You are terrific at selling things and do extremely well in all retail fields especially consumer goods, beauty products and fashion.

You are playful, warm and sweet which means that you are a popular boy or girl and can count many as your friends. You enjoy people and have a forgiving nature; you cannot take unpleasantness and will avoid confrontation. You are not an aggressive person and use your charm, intellect and strong will to get where you want to be. You are very competitive secretly and can exhibit a rather jealous streak at times. You are adept at money management and excel in all financial careers.

Beauty and art mean a great deal to you and even if you pursue a career in something not very arty, you will fill your free time pursuing creative hobbies, decorating or buying nice things. You are very talented artistically and have an eye for proportion, colour and form. You enjoy poetry and music and appreciate these things more than just superficially.

You are liberal in your attitudes and take a progressive approach to relationships. You are fair minded and will fight for justice for friends and strangers.

Worldly success matters to you and so does love. You will not want to live the single life for long and will crave a stable and physically satisfying love relationship. You are highly sensual and have a strong sex drive. You will sacrifice quite a bit for harmony in relationships as you hate discord, but you should never turn yourself inside out to make another happy – it's two way street.

Refined and always well-presented you like to look good and appearances matter to you. You are loving and have depths of sympathy and concern for others. You will often strive to keep relationships with old friends going long after they have broken down, you always look to build bridges and you never forget a good deed. You make for a loyal and consistent friend and lover who has a depth of feeling and can be rather intense. You are rarely without a string of admirers. Your challenge in life is to know when to let go – no more flogging dead horses, some people or places or jobs have a time and a place and you need to know when to move on.

You are very good at starting businesses and finding ways to make money. You like putting your efforts into things which pay off in a concrete way. You have some very quirky habits and peculiar preferences. You can earn money via your creative gifts and ability to get on with people.

You believe life should be enjoyed and you have fun loving personality.

While intensely jealous and moved to anger when the green-eyed monster strikes, June 6's are generally pacifists. You can be materialistic and are motivated by money for the beautiful things which it can buy. 6 June's are often collectors or dealers in art or jewellery. You do not let go easily and are deeply hurt when relationships or friendships turn sour. You are skilled at negotiation and you do well in marriage counselling or where you can resolve disputes. You are very diplomatic and fair and yet can be tougher than you look – when your stubborn side kicks in you can be anything but docile and passive.

Money can be earned from your talents in design, diplomacy, and hospitality or in the arts. June 6's are often good at accumulating money and tend to be prosperous. You make a good manager in industries where people are a key resource as opposed to technology. You are good at business, law and accounting. June 6's often inherit money or earn much of their wealth early in life. You can spend as much as you earn extravagantly, so you are not always a good saver. In some cases June 6 can become very mean and hoard money and wealth for money's sake.

When June 6's feel strongly about something, they will express their opinions with zeal and can be very persuasive. You enjoy the cut and thrust of debate and you often win as you are highly logical and very practical in your approach.

Those born this day are highly effective combining a keen intellect, social skills and graces and artistic talent.

Famous people born this day: Diego Velazquez, Bjorn Borg, Sandra Bernhard, Thomas Mann, Amanda Pays.

1887 J.S. Pemberton's Coca-Cola label was trademark registered.

JUNE 7

Ruling planets are Mercury and Neptune.

Lucky colours are the darker green shades.

Lucky gems are turquoise, cats eye chrysoberyl, tigers eye.

Highly imaginative and musical those born this day have a deeply spiritual and private side. They are very sensitive to the needs and feelings of others and have a compassionate and caring nature. You are very self-sacrificing and seek meaning through devotion to a course or person. Medicine and healing is very strong theme for this day and many nurses, doctors, pharmacists and alternative healing practitioners are born this day.

You are lucky in life as you know how to use your powers of deduction, observation and intuition to time your moves just right. You can be shrewd in business although you do not find making money fulfilling; you find evolving via love and art most satisfying. You explore life via your imagination and enjoy travelling much for the reason that it stimulates the imagination and allows you to escape.

You are very stubborn and tend to attract others who have that trait meaning that relationships can be tricky and with neither of you willing to back down, problems can spiral with stalemates becoming unbearable. You delight in travel to far flung places and favour sea travel and places by the sea. You are restless and moody and enjoy retreating from the madden crowd to places of seclusion. You have a strong need to pursue spiritual goals and find that artistic expression and music gets you more in touch with your higher self and a feeling of destiny. You have very unique ideas about religion and yet everything you do is marked by compassion and the ability to make sacrifices for those you love or those less fortunate. You need to balance your needs with this need to help others or you may actually become a victim of those you seek to help. You must learn to be more discerning in terms of your actions towards others – you cannot save everyone and you may sometimes be taken advantage of.

Many on this day have a natural ability to heal and can excel at healing techniques which require hands on ie massage therapy, reflexology, physiotherapy and chiropracting.

You are a dark horse and a hard person to know as you are very deep and keep much of yourself hidden from view.

Money is key to this day and you have the ability to achieve great wealth – you will seek to do good things with this money. It is hard for you to fail where money is concerned and you excel at merchant banking, trading and marketing. You have a strong sense of universal obligation and enjoy using your fame and your money to shine the spotlight on those less fortunate or on causes close to your heart. You are keen on children's charities and those which support the disabled. Less evolved people on this date can be ruthless and extremely calculating and deceptive in amassing money.

Those born on June 7 must always be on guard against scams and liars as your giving nature can make your vulnerable to deception. You can be highly idealistic in love and are often disappointed as you cannot see the failings in the people you spoil with your affections. You want to save people but need to be aware that while you can assist, at the end of the day others have to want to help themselves.

Disappointments in love are some of the most transformative events for you and you often find these periods artistically inspiring.

June 7 political leaders often feel divinely inspired in what they do – although delusion can mean their actions in reality are far from divine at all. June 7's can rise to the very heights of self-sacrifice and service above self or sink to the lowest levels of deceit and depravity.

June 7 has an association with the sea and many love to live near the sea front or work as oceanographers, sailors, sea conservationists or water sportsmen. June 7's have wanderlust and yet they have an enduring need for an anchor – they must have a constant in their life, something or someone they can rely on or else their innate insecurity and fear of the future can be unbearable. This may mean you travel in youth when you still have a home with your parents or later in life when you have saved for a nest egg.

You are motivated by people, beauty and ideals more than by money and yet can make a great deal of money in your specialist fields. More at home in theatres, galleries, far flung places or working directly with people than in the boardroom, you like to be hands on.

Your ambitions fluctuate and you do not often discuss them with with others – most of your ambitious have a philosophical motivation.

Famous people born this day: Prince, Liam Neeson, Tom Jones, Dean Martin, Muammar Gadaffi, Anna Kournikova, Anne McLain, Paul Gauguin and Jessica Tandy.

1946 "Eensie Weensie Spider" by Yola De Meglio was copyright registered.
1953 The first colour network telecast in compatible colour was broadcast from a station in Boston.

JUNE 8

Ruling planets are Mercury and Saturn.

Lucky colours are deep blue and black.

Lucky gems are blue sapphire, lapis lazuli and amethyst.

You are a workaholic and an excellent networker. Insatiability curious, versatile, trend setting and stylish you thrive on challenges. You have a dramatic flair and are ambitious and driven. Very witty, current and aware of what is going on in the world you are often the first to capitalize on a trend. You know how to make an idea into a money spinner and have excellent business acumen.

You have a cautious, serious side and can be cynical about the motivations of others. However you are also highly organised and systematic in your thinking and are great with numbers and financial matters. You accumulate wealth as you are ambitious and because you know how business works – you are a very practical person.

Honest and down to earth you have a much greater dose of staying power than the average Gemini and are determined and persevering. You can be a little negative at times and in your youth you may lack confidence in yourself, but like everything in your life, you work at things and confidence grows. You have a solid sense of purpose and can commit to goals with clear focus and sustained effort. June 8 achieve much and yet they often do it quietly. You make a very formidable opponent as you are highly resourceful and you keep at it.

In relationships you look for sensible and stable partners and may marry someone older. You like commitment and are not a person who enjoys casual relationships. Loyal and trustworthy you take responsibility and obligation seriously.

You have a strong need to protect yourself and you are wary of others and their motivations. June 8's are strong characters and yet you can be plagued by feelings of inadequacy, it may take you time to fully develop and understand your talents and know how to use them. Confidence comes with age and experience and you go from strength to strength. It is common that a June 8 is dominated by a male family member or possibly suffers restriction in early life due to cultural or economic influences. June 8's can become obsessed with getting even with their past and almost having their own back; there is a strong drive to live life to the full to make up for something you feel you missed in childhood or adolescence. Over compensation can be a problem for June 8 and it can lead you on to paths that seem fulfilling but are not. Life is not a tick box exercise, you should concentrate on discovering what truly fulfils you and not spending time doing what society says or following current trends.

You are a worrier and need to learn how to let go and quieten that voice in your head that is always criticising you or making you feel guilty.

You are neither pushy nor showy, in fact you are reserved although when you get going you have a dry sense of humour that can crack others up. You tend to be very modest and you go about your business in a quiet unobtrusive way. You are highly law abiding may pursue careers in the police or in law. Your shyness and reserve is often a cover for a deeply sensitive and insecure side which you like to keep hidden. You are intensely ambitious and driven to overcome limitations and to succeed. You are happiest when you are working to prove something to yourself rather than to others. You tend to do very well in trades or professions and are best starting out with a trade and a profession. Business usually attracts June 8 in the end. June 8's make good lawyers, accountants, financial planners, bankers and are often successful in the tough world of politics.

June 8 can make informed and rational decisions under high pressure and you rarely lose your focus. You like to focus and work on something specific; you work less well in fast moving work environments with lots of disruptions. You like to make order from chaos. You are known for your high integrity and will usually steer well clear of what is dubious or pie in the sky.

June 8 often have to struggle with poor health in childhood and yet as adults they are robust and tend to have longevity. Often the poor health in childhood is to do with poor diet or emotional stress due to the home or social circumstances; when June 8's are older and in control of their lives they thrive. June 8 cannot be dominated or you will get very depressed; you must be in control. Sometimes June 8's are perceived as controlling – this can be due to your need to guard against the un-foreseen and to be prepared. Like all good scouts and guides, June 8 like to be prepared.

June 8's can often be tormented by 'what if's' and pursued by guilt, but they need to give themselves a break and let up on the self-criticism and work on fostering self-love. 8's need to learn that it is not a sin to have fun.

Famous people on this day: Joan Rivers, Bonnie Tyler, Nancy Sinatra, Tim Berners Lee, Barbara Bush, Mick Hucknell, Francis Crick, Boz Scaggs, Kanye West and Mary King.

1869 Ives McGaffey patented a carpet sweeping machine. This was the first patent for a device that cleaned rugs.

JUNE 9

Ruling planets are Mercury and Mars.

Lucky colours are red, maroon and scarlet and autumnal tones.

Lucky gems are red coral and garnet.

June 9 is a go-getter. Active, passionate and impulsive, you are a highly motivated person whose life is exciting and dynamic. You are determined and proactive and will not let life pass you by, you are always looking to open doors and make things happen. You are very strong willed and have a mind of your own, you like to lead and resent being told what to do. Highly impatient, you have a temper and routine and restriction get you down. Headstrong and independent you strike out on your own from early on and have a strong purpose.

You enjoy being first and revel in being the first one to try something new. Novelty excites you and you will try anything once. Incredibly curious and rather gung ho, you will be the one to get the ball rolling. You have a very capable mind and learn fast; you are skilled with numbers and at sports. Physically you are fit and active.

Due to your enthusiasm, positive attitude and natural inclination to grab opportunities without thinking twice you will find success and wealth. You are not driven by money, but you enjoy all the opportunities money affords you. You can come across as bossy and sometimes your words are too blunt, but you are an honest and straight-talking person. Fast and efficient, you get the job done.

You hate laziness and passive people; you love to work and enjoy being busy. Physical activity is a great outlet for your energy and a good way to relax. You are competitive and highly skilful in terms of sports and physical activity. You may also excel at working with cars, machinery or weapons and engineering is a wonderful field for you to go into.

You may be attracted into politics in later life and due to the unique spiritual vibration of this day, you may be able to affect far reaching social change.

You are creative and fired up, but you must learn to direct your anger more productively and see tasks through to conclusions. You are excellent at starting things, but less good at taking things through to a successful conclusion – thus you work well with others who have the ability to hammer out details and take plans thru to the final stages.

You can be domineering and exacting; you are very good at managing material assets. You know the value of things and drive a hard bargain. Your timing in terms of buying material assets is excellent. You may also excel at business restructuring.

You have the ability to overcome all obstacles and be victorious over your competitors. You are blessed in that others will usually place their trust and confidence in you; giving you a leg up in terms of personal advancement. You will always act with honesty and in good faith even to your own detriment. You can be trusted with funds held in trust or as a treasurer.

June 9 will take on a dare and often you can be a little naive and can be cajoled into things which are detrimental. You often act then think and your impulsiveness opens doors for you as well as getting you in trouble.

June 9's are quite vulnerable although they look invincible. June 9's inspire others and have great leadership ability. Although not stubborn, June 9 will work hard to achieve anything they set their sights on and yet their goals can change over time, meaning they sometimes abandon one thing to jump on the next bandwagon. Sometimes you lack the follow through as you get bored and want to move on to the next big thing. June 9's are better starters than finishers. You often make snap decisions, but you act on gut feel and instinct and this can often mean you make good choices without overthinking things.

You have a temper, it will flare up quickly and die down just as fast; when angry you will speak your mind, which may offend more sensitive or diplomatic types, you are however honest and are not given to grudge bearing. You are very trusting and this can be your downfall, you assume others are as honest and upfront as you are. June 9's are an open book – you find it hard to keep secrets about yourself. June 9 are direct and to the point and yet they are seldom malicious, but honest. You are seldom devious or underhand; you go for what you want in an open way.

You must have independence, you work better when you are your own boss or where you have freedom to make decisions. You are not a good follower and can be disruptive if you do not have power. You make up your own mind and will not be bossed about.

You need to learn to be more discerning and more cynical about the motives of others and you need to learn to think before you speak.

June 9 will never let doubts or fears stop them living and loving life. You have a giant lust for everything in this life and very little gets you down for long.

Generous and often spendthrift, you make money not for money's sake, but for the opportunities it offers to do more, experience more and learn more. You love to give and to take those you love on the adventure of life with you.

Famous people born this day: Jonny Depp, Michael J Fox, Natalie Portman, Miroslav Klose, Jackie Mason, Les Paul and Cole Porter.

1953 Patent #2,641,545 was granted to John Kraft for the "manufacture of soft surface cured cheese"

JUNE 10

Ruling planets are Mercury and the Sun.

Lucky colours are copper and gold.

Lucky gem is Ruby.

With an excellent mind and strong will, you are going places. You can lead and also work independently quite happily. Mentally dexterous and agile you can adapt to most environments and you learn fast. You can use your creativity with great success in business and you can also excel in the world of the performing arts. You have good people skills and are able to relate to people on some level no matter where they come from – you are rarely intimidated and are at ease in most situations.

You believe in love and will make great sacrifices for those you love. It is in love that you are most idealistic.

You are disciplined and have a sense of direction and purpose. Sometimes you can come across as arrogant and opinionated and you do need to be more flexible and compromising in your thinking and actions.

Self-expression is vital to your psychology, if you are in a situation where you cannot be yourself or express that creativity and joie de vivre you have, you will suffer physically. You have to have independence and a chance to live your own life on your own terms and be expansive emotionally and spiritually. You wither in situations that are highly controlling or prescriptive.

You gravitate to positions in life where you can lead or shine in some way. You are an inspiring person who will always attract attention. In general your health is excellent and you have strong powers of recuperation. You must get fresh air, sunlight and physical activity is vital for you. Usually being active physically and doing sports, dance or something energetic is a major part of your life.

You communicate extremely effectively and can excel in writing, public speaking, acting, PR, speech writing or in the press. This is a day of power and accomplishment with the warning that the spoils can be squandered on frivolous and impulsive activities.

Your life will follow cycles of 5 or 7 years with sudden dramatic changes altering your life course after these periods. Your early life is filled with change and often changes of residence; you crave your own home and when you do afford it you will decorate superbly and enjoy entertaining there. Your home is your castle.

Your life swings from side to side – when you are doing well financially you tend to fail in love and visa versa. It is a challenge for you to create balance and stability in all aspects of life.

June 10 is associated with rise and fall and reversals of fortune. Your name will be known for good or evil and it is down to you and your desire. You are capable of engendering passionate responses from others in terms of love, hate, fear or respect. There is often little middle ground with you, but you must own everything you do and realise that every outcome is in your hands.

Your ability to visualise and actualise is strong and thus positive thinking and neurolinguistic programming techniques can be very effective for you. This comes with the caveat of: be careful of what you wish for – you can achieve anything you want, but make sure you know what you really want and make choices wisely or your very success can become an albatross.

Learning self-discipline and compassion are your challenges, you can be self-centred at times and while you are highly sensitive and caring to those closest to you, you do need to cultivate more compassion for those beyond your immediate circle.

You can be very single minded in pursuing goals and often cannot see the wood for the trees – you need to think of wider implications. June 10 who fail to gain authority and power and who cannot find an outlet for their creative abilities can become resentful, deeply frustrated and self-destructive. Sometimes a proud and arrogant manner is your way of coping with insecurity.

June 10's often have leadership thrust upon them as people turn to you in crisis and when tough decisions must be made. You are generous and warm hearted exhibiting concern for others. You have a very strong attachment to identity and often identify with nationality or religion very vehemently. Criticism is not welcomed because is often deemed as a personal affront as you are invested in what you are and proud of what you are, that pride is sometimes too easily wounded. Having respect is important to June 10's who enjoy organising and taking control of people and situations.

You enjoy the limelight and are often attracted to performing arts – you may well have a shy side and yet externally you are gregarious and outgoing. You can be flamboyant and enjoy being known for your style and pazzaz. You usually know when a June 10 walks into the room as you radiate energy and take the room by storm. You are unlikely to ever be a wall flower; although you can be very private person, you know how to manage a very public façade.

Famous people born this day: Judy Garland, Prince Phillip Duke of Edinburgh, Liz Hurley, Carlo Ancelotti, Gina Gershon, Jeanne Tripplehorn and Maurice Sendak.

1952 The polyester film MYLAR was trademark registered.
1902 A patent for the "window envelope" for letters was granted to H.F. Callahan.

JUNE 11

Ruling planets and Mercury and Moon.

Your lucky colours are cream and white and green.

Your lucky gems are moonstone or pearl.

Intelligent and smart you are a person who knows how to make their way in the world and who uses a combination of logic and intuition to make decisions. You have wanderlust and enjoy travelling to new places and ringing the changes in your life. You are never fearful of change and you embrace it; you adapt well to most circumstances and get along with people.

You are a firm friend who maintains her ties with the past and nurtures relationships. While you like to ring the changes you will never neglect what is important and will always protect certain parts of your life from the ravages of change. You like to form strong bonds with others as you are a sensitive soul who likes to retreat to the loving protective arms of a lover, family or friend. You need to be understood and can be frustrated when you are not listened to and when others cannot be bothered to understand your emotions.

You have strong beliefs and will stand up for them with courage and conviction. You are sentimental and a romantic who believes in true love and the value of commitment. You are in typical Gemini style very unpredictable and can often surprise others by making sudden decisions. You have courage and a very pragmatic way of dealing with life. You will spoil those you love and are very thoughtful, sympathetic and kind. You do not suffer fools gladly and cannot tolerate those who are perpetually woeful and will not help themselves.

You are a cheerful person, but can be dragged down if you are with toxic and negative people as you absorb the emotions around you. You are good with your money and do not like to be indebted. You value financial independence greatly. You cannot be contained or restricted or you will rebel. You can be very dramatic when you get emotional.

You have a tender heart and yet you do not let anyone and everyone know that. You have an excellent ability to write, especially about your emotional experiences. You get on well with women and can find that it is women more than men who can be of help to you career-wise and emotionally. You can be moody and there are times when you will have spells of depression – the best way to tackle these bouts of the blues is via physical activity. You may even be surprised at yourself when you plummet into these depths – you are always being surprised by yourself and your life is a journey of learning to know yourself as you are a very complex person.

You have a strong sense of purpose and destiny and the ability to uplift yourself and others with the force of your personality and leading by example. You are one to rise to the occasion no matter what your level of confidence.

Money is not your main motivator and once you are secure and comfortable you will focus more on emotionally driven goals rather than money accumulation. Acquiring knowledge is not always easy for June 11 and they may be too restless or even nervy to settle and do well at school. You learn by osmosis and the university of life is your best teacher. That said, you also learn by reading voraciously and via talking to others. You are very canny and good at working out solutions.

You often rely on your personality to give you a break career-wise but you should never underestimate your skills and language skills. It is always important for you to save money for a rainy day and financial performances can fluctuate.

Famous people born this day: Gene Wilder, Dappy, Caroline Quentin, Jackie Stewart, Jacques Cousteau, Richard Strauss, Shia LaBeouf, Joshua Jackson, Hugh Laurie, Peter Dinklage.

1895 Charles Duryea patented a gasoline powered automobile.

JUNE 12

Ruling planets are Mercury and Jupiter.

Your lucky colours are yellow, lemon and sandy shades.

Your lucky gems are yellow sapphire, citrine quartz and golden topaz.

You have excellent communication skills and are able to convey ideas in a way that is entertaining and inspiring. You have the ability to spark interest in others and create a buzz around what you believe in.

Curious, adventurous, open minded and seeking of answers and enlightenment. You are excellent at writing and communicating in a way which is interesting and engaging. When you speak people listen and you have the power to influence and get a message across.

Sociable and popular you make for a great conversationalist and you are able to get on with people from all walks of life. You can become bored and moody very quickly when you do not get enough mental stimulation or stimulation from your surroundings – you enjoy fast paced dynamic people-friendly workplaces or working outdoors. You can however end up chasing your tail and achieving little due to your need to keep moving, you must spend more time looking inwards and learning about your needs, desires and using these as an indicator of your true purpose and destiny. You are capable of great commitment to a worthwhile cause and you can make a difference to others, or you can chose the route of party animal, where life is one long social where all commitment is avoided.

While you are very impressive in terms of a speaker or promoter you may need to temper some of your opinions and learn some moderation, as at times you may come across as over the top. Do not feel the need to exaggerate, just stick to the facts and let your enthusiasm for your beliefs do the talking. You can be very effective in giving leadership in any area where parties are looking to resolve disputes or find common ground. You make a great negotiator, sales person and diplomat.

Communication and variety is vital in your emotional and personal life and you may well marry more than once. You need to be with someone who is just as communicative and responsive as you, if you are with someone who is not enthusiastic and who does not like to take life by the scruff of the neck and live it, you can become very frustrated. The strong silent type is not for you. While a practical and stable partner can do you good, you still need someone with a common zest for life and idealistic approach.

You are a flamboyant person who loves to think big, you love a bit of razzmatazz and are partial to pomp and ceremony – you can see why politics attracts people on this day.

The more you see money as a means and not an ends the better you tend to do in terms of financial wealth. Your biggest challenges in terms of financial security can come from health issues, children or via your partner's finances and so you would do well to take insurance where possible to mitigate these factors.

You can be very successful if you choose your course and stick to it. You are dynamic when you have found a place in life where you can lose yourself and contribute in a worthwhile way. While you love change and variety, uncertainty can dog you – you like changes when you are in control of them and are not as adaptable when the changes are in control of you.

Be on guard that you do not construct a separate reality that is not in tune with actual reality.

Those born on this day should watch their back; the number 12 warns of downfall due to dishonesty and unreliability from those around you who are not as trustworthy as they seem. It may be the case that you prove a fall guy in someone else's ambitious desire to get ahead. Be alert to your circumstances and be wary of those who seek to flatter; be slow to trust new friends. Always be sceptical of those who offer you something which on the surface seems highly desirable – what are their true motives? Always be aware of those in your life who want to use you to get ahead – no harm in having your eyes open.

Sometimes those born on this day fail to learn by mistakes: while sometimes things are different the second time, often in life things didn't work for a reason the first time and we need to accept that and leave some things/people alone for good.

You make a wise and perceptive teacher and counsellor to others and yet as clearly as you can see others' problems and are able to guide them, you are not always able to see your own issues with such perspective and would do well to take good advice from someone trusted.

You are a seeker and someone with a thirst for knowledge; you will sacrifice much to gain knowledge or a great education. You need to pay more attention to your emotions and the inner voice. Do not always chose your head over your heart.

With age, you become a wise philosopher who rarely grows old and bitter – in fact you always retain a youthful spirit. June 12 will always be a dreamer working on some goal. Many June 12's who cannot study further at a young age, achieve in academia later in life.

Law and education are excellent careers for you as they provide a springboard for your missions in terms of society, justice and leadership.

Famous people born this day: Anne Frank, George Herbert Walker Bush ie Bush Snr, Charles Kingsley, Jason Mewes.

1928 The brightly coloured, candy-coated, licorice candy, Good and Plenty was trademark registered.

JUNE 13

Ruling planets are Mercury and Uranus.

Lucky colours are electric blue, white and multi-colors.

Lucky gems are Hessonite garnet and agate.

Your nature can be a touch tricky to understand as while your need for change and constant stimulation is marked, you also have a strong need to stability and a certain routine. Quick witted, intellectual, progressive and curious you enjoy people and debate and may well be politically minded. You are clever with maths and can be very at home in scientific fields. You enjoy learning, although study per se may bore you. Often June 13 do not fulfil their promise at school as you get bored very easily and may not be able to concentrate for long. You learn best when it is on your own terms in a field you love. Technology is your forte and you are gifted in the emerging technical fields.

You will go through many transformations in your life often prompted by events that come out of the blue. You are fascinated by the unknown and enjoy anything new: new ideas, new frontiers, new research. You enjoy work and excel when you have a project you are committed to from an intellectual and philosophical standpoint.

Highly creative, you pride yourself on your originality and ability to come up with unique solutions.

You are a warm and magnanimous person who gives off a lot of energy, in fact you are often totally shattered and depleted as you burn the candle at both ends. You need to learn more moderation for the sake of your nerves. You live for the moment working hard and playing hard and you do not often pay enough heed to your health. You need to have a more balanced diet and get more quality nutrition. You need to find ways to relax unwind and switch off effectively.

Although you will always be busy and surrounded by people you can often feel isolated. You crave a strong one to one bond with someone who may not necessarily be you love partner per se. You are always seeking a divine connection to someone and it may elude you as what you really need is to find is yourself – a deep and true respect and understanding of who and what you are. Learning to not only love, but also to understand and value yourself is a challenge for you.

The more you work diligently and constructively the more luck will come your way. Work and being productive is extremely important to you. A life of leisure is not part of the divine plan for this date of birth and if you avoid responsibility and hide from duty and work, you may face ruin.

While you benefit from the structure work, family and society give you, you are prone to rebel against and resent these very things – don't always bite the hand which feeds you.

While material things do motivate you, you have a strong spiritual seeking inclination which you should not ignore. Hard work can make any dream you have reality.

The number 13 is not unlucky, it is associated with change, upheaval and new opportunity. Those born on this day should always look to the future and not the past and should embrace change and grab the possibilities it offers. You have access to much power which if used unselfishly can bring credit to you and positive change to others.

June 13 is a day of the unexpected, be prepared for change and be adaptable, as it is during times of change you discover most about your potential. The number 13 is associated with genius and also with explorers and new discoveries.

This is a day of thinking out of the box and going with the winds of change as an agent of that change and never a soldier of the old guard.

June 13 may include artists and philosophers who are not recognised or appreciated in their time; they often face ridicule or censorship, even imprisonment as their ideas may not be accepted in their lifetime.

Science and especially outer space are topics which fascinate June 13 – you may research aliens, crop circles, UFO's or conspiracies.

Human rights, women's lib and green issues are causes which June 13 get passionate about and you espouse tolerance and equality although strangely enough you can fall foul of an ivory tower mentality failing to follow through on your high ideals.

You have a large amount of acquaintances, but few true friends. You are actually introverted emotionally and reveal your true feelings only to those you trust or with whom you feel a spiritual connection.

Famous people born on this day: Ban Ki-Moon, John Forbes Nash, William Yeats, Mary-Kate and Ashley Olsen, Paul Lynde, Malcolm McDowell, Tim Allen.

1944 Patent #2,351,004 was granted to Marvin Camras for the magnetic tape recorder.

JUNE 14

Ruling planets is Mercury.

Lucky color is green.

Lucky gems are Emerald, Aquamarine or Jade.

A fun, bright, optimistic person who gets on well with everyone and adds spice to life. You are positive and quirky with a good sense of humour.

Quick witted, curious, versatile and impulsive. Your nature has many contradictions and you enjoy having a sense of security and predictability more than you realise. At times unreliable and at other times passionately committed you can be a little erratic and you confuse others as much as you excite and intrigue them. You enjoy people and are socially driven. You love to be surrounded by people and enjoy the ambiance of coming and going. You are a fast learner and eager to try new things and jump into new experiences.

Influential writing, communication and use of the media is part and parcel of this day. You have a magnetism that helps draw people to you and aids you in getting your message across. In business and partnerships you will undergo many changes over a lifetime and change will nearly always bring something positive.

You get bored fast and crave new pastures. You enjoy news, current affairs and anything where you receive information as information is your life blood. You are not someone who likes to take it easy and let life pass you by, you want to be there in the thick of the action.

You express yourself well and tend to know the right word for the right moment. You are quick to spot errors and you will point those out. You can be very critical and often very to the point which can seem harsh to sensitive signs, however you see anything that is factual as fair game for comment. The freedom to be polite is really no freedom at all and you reserve the right to point out what is obvious. You may often lack some self-confidence as you are also keenly aware of your own faults and the mistakes you make. You dislike being inaccurate are always conscientious especially in your work.

June 14 crave the stimulation of travel and new people and places. Your life is full of short journeys and longer ones whenever possible. You change residence often and may rent rather than buy for the freedom that offers. When you outgrow something you move on – no regrets, you take everything life throws at you as an experience to learn from.

You enjoy being constructive and you like working on big, long terms goals where you see something i.e. an idea or a business growing and evolving over time. You love a good deal and are a master of driving a hard bargain – you love to haggle be it in the boardroom or in a market in Bangkok. You are very adept at processing information, you know your facts and how to use them and you are skilled at applying knowledge with common sense. You are a thinker and you know that the pen is mightier than the sword.

You are talented at picking up skills and may well speak more than 3 languages. You don't like to be tied down and reserve the right to change your mind at any time and you often do.

You are good at seeing both sides of the coin which can make you very effective in business and politics and you get where the other guy is coming from and can see their weaknesses.

Your enthusiasm is never in question, but you do need to be a little more patient and to be more consistent in your efforts which can be all or nothing at times. With age you will be less likely to go off on tangents and more able to focus on what really matters. You are devoted to your ideals and have a love of life that will help you get through anything.

Those on June 14 get many lucky breaks and have a great shot at being financially comfortable in life. You are devoted and loyal to those you love, but perhaps you need to let them know that – you are often not great at expressing feelings of love and need to be more comfortable about displaying emotion.

Uncertainty is a big issue for this day, you have an inbuilt desire to build security and will invest or insure to guard against financial uncertainty. It is possible that in your late teens and early twenties you will fall foul of unreliable or dishonest friends or partners. If you are attractive, talented or wealthy; jealousy from others can be a big hurdle to overcome and the source of some problems for you. Avoid gossip yourself and never let being the subject of idle gossip bother you.

Early marriage is often riven with pitfalls and you should delay marriage until your late 20' at least. You may travel in order to report on or participate in social change, reform or national politics.

Speculation on the basis of facts and logic can be very lucky for you although gambling on chance should be avoided. Financial stability must be protected and never take for granted.

The number 14 contains within it danger related to the natural world ie floods, hurricanes, earthquakes and tornados – so always be cautious and insure if necessary.

Always check the facts for yourself and be careful that people do not misrepresent the facts to convince you of anything. Reliance on others in general is a mistake and you should trust your own judgement and intuition. Over-confidence and impatience can be your undoing.

Famous people born this day: Donald Trump, Boy George, Che Guevara, Alan Carr, Harriet Beecher Stowe, Steffi Graf, Paul O' Grady, Rowan Williams, Val Valentino and Ray Luzier.

1927 George Washington Carver received a patent for a process of producing paints and stains.

JUNE 15

Ruling planets are Mercury and Venus.

Lucky colours are white and cream, rose and pink.

Lucky gems are diamond, white sapphire or quartz crystal.

This day is associated with eloquence, good communicative ability and the gifts of music, drama and art. It is a very lucky day and gives those born on the 15th a dramatic flair and magnetic personality.

You are highly personable, warm and entertaining. You are a pleasure to be around and make for a very lively and fun companion. Highly diplomatic and courteous you like to be polite and friendly and you get things done by co-operation rather than conflict which you avoid at all costs. You are a born entertainer and are very talented in the arts. Usually those on this day discover their artistic talents early on and are supported by their family in pursuing them.

You are a team player and you are a very inclusive person who does not like to hurt another's feelings. There is a youthful quality about you no matter how old you are. Highly creative and very artistic you are drawn to the arts in career or as a hobby.

Partnership is very important to you and you will not live the single life for long, many on this day marry childhood sweethearts. You enjoy working in a team or in a partnership and you work well with money and in business. No matter what career you chose you will bring a fair minded attitude and a strong business acumen to play. You are highly persuasive and make a great negotiator or sales person.

While you crave relationships and love, your independent streak may mean that relationships do not always run smoothly as you would like. Your partner will have to embrace and acknowledge your need for freedom and to be spontaneous. You are a flirt and cannot survive with a jealous and possessive type. Your partner must also realise that your friends are important to you, as is your work – you are a person with ambitions.

You are a very modern person with progressive values and a love of fashion and anything exciting and trendy. Material things delight you and yet you are also a person who values people and you make for a very loving and generous family member.

It is likely that your 24th birthday will be the start of something significant.

You have a significant amount of power socially and you can use that to 'win friends and influence people' as they say – this power is vital to get ahead in politics or any career where networking and contacts are important.

You have an abiding fear of not having enough money, financial security can even become an obsession for you. You are very money conscious and although you enjoy spending, debt worries the life out of you. June 15 people are very good at finding sponsors and backers to help them financially as you have a very strong personal magnetism.

One of your challenges is dealing with your tendency to become fixated on things and people to the point that you lose perspective. Sometimes you let things get too far and are actually relieved when someone or something steps in and brings it all crashing down – you end up wondering how it ever got that far in the first place. Often you struggle to change course or put the brakes on when things get going.

Those born on this day should never dabble in the occult for negative purposes and any foray into these fields should be with caution.

You need to challenge yourself to keep pushing for perfection – June 15 can be complacent and as luck usually runs with those born on this day, you may ride on that luck and begin to rely on it rather than driving to better yourself and excel even more.

Those born on this day make excellent traders and buyers of beauty products, consumer good and fashion.

This day contains an extremely fortunate vibration which is enhanced even further when used to do good to others.

Famous people born on this day: Courteney Cox, Helen Hunt, Neil Patrick Harris, Jim Belushi, Nadine Coyle, Demis Roussos, Noddy Holder, Michael Laudrup, Errol Garner and Ana Torv.

1844 Charles Goodyear was granted patent #3,633 for vulcanized rubber.

JUNE 16

Ruling planets are Mercury and Neptune.

Lucky colours are the darker green shades.

Lucky gems are turquoise, cats' eye chrysoberyl, tigers eye.

Those born this day have an incredible imagination, high ideals and personal appeal. You are somewhat illusive and mysterious and have a youthful quality throughout your life. June 16 people are true visionaries. You are able to use your intuition and verbal skills to be highly persuasive and although you are not a pushy person you have a subtle way of putting pressure on others to steer them in a direction you want. You use your power subtly.

Musical ability, medicine and travel are strongly indicated for this day. Air hostesses, ship captains, singers, composers, paramedics, nurses and doctors are some common careers.

You are a day dreamer and may be highly disorganised, you need time alone to be with your thoughts and you thrive when you get sufficient rest and relaxation. Techniques like yoga and meditation are highly beneficial to you. You are a person who absorbs the emotions of those around you and you need time alone to centre yourself and get in touch with your true needs and values. This is one of the most emotional days in Gemini and also represents a very sensitive and compassionate person. Things affect you deeply and you find it hard to shake the unpleasant things in life off, although you do always learn from them.

You often have prophetic dreams or sudden flashes of insight; you are psychic and a good judge of character. You may also have lucid dreams or even experiences where you see ghosts or have other worldly experiences. Your dreams are extremely vivid and are often a form of escapism or even part of your job i.e. authors, film directors, photographers, script writers, poets and song writers. You enjoy dream interpretation and find it useful. You tend to dream more than most and those dreams can have an effect on you.

June 16 have a keen interest in anything esoteric: symbolism, mythology, space, religious mysticism, taboos, mysteries and conspiracies. Many of you have the gift i.e. are clairvoyant, clairaudient or psychic.

Addictive behaviour is common with this day and so you are best avoiding gambling, alcohol and other substances and staying well clear of friends and partners who do use them.

You are very restless and enjoy travel and any activity connected with the sea. You love to share your ideas with others and it is via music, art, poetry and dance that you can do this highly effectively. You are a romantic who seeks a soul mate who can provide an anchor, stability and be on a par with you spiritually.

You can be highly critical, sarcastic, impatient and irritable when you are unfocused or depressed. You can experience fluctuating moods which are often quite baffling to others and even yourself. You have a very deep side which remains hidden most of the time and you have a strong need for self-protection. When you feel trapped you will slip away from a situation: sometimes retreating or even running away from things is how you deal best with them.

Your personality is highly fluid and you will undergo many changes in your life; like a chameleon you take on the colour of your environment which can be a great thing if that environment is positive and supportive and very negative if the opposite is the case. In adult life you must choose your associates and friends carefully and always avoid toxic people whose negative emotions can bring you down. Being with the wrong people can cause you to be depressed and almost emotionally paralysed where you spiral downwards finding it hard to break free.

Water has a magical power over you and has an emotionally healing and balancing quality.

You are a very compassionate person who can be incredibly selfless and self-sacrificing when devoting your life to a cause you believe in. Medical fields attract you as does religious and charitable work. You are highly curious about mystical and spiritual matters and may visit clairvoyants and psychics. June 16 people are rather psychic themselves and some may look to make this a career.

In business and the theatrical world your contacts are vital to you and are a closely guarded secret. Those on this day often like to keep secrets and play their cards close to their chest.

June 16 people can be incredibly successful due to their charisma and ability to manipulate situations subtly.

There can be many disappointments and sacrifices made in love and although those on this day may experience real love and true passion it may not run smoothly. "The closer you get to the fire the more you get burned." Affairs and secret lovers are a possibility.

When money is not the aim, but when you are inspired by the love of what you do, then money and fame will come your way; if greed and materialism are your motivation, you will never find true happiness.

There is a fatalistic side to the destiny of this day – unavoidable lessons must be learned. You are advised to always make plans in advance and to make sure you plans are as solid as possible, always have a plan B to fall back on and never be complacent. Always listen to the voice within, learn to understand your intuition and follow it. Pay heed to dreams which may warn you of something.

Fame and leadership can bring added complications to the life of June 16 in terms of a heavier karma, this can be avoided by those who live a normal life.

You are highly empathetic and have an intuitive understanding of other's emotions – you work well in the caring professions where patience and compassion are key. You tend to carry the problems of others on your back and in your heart, you worry much about those you love and the state of the world. You are a confidante and counsellor to your friends – you offer a shoulder to cry on and wise words to soothe and calm. June 16 are very private people and can be a great mystery to others as you hold much close to your chest. You rarely share your own problems with others. You will avoid what is judgmental or unduly harsh, you are not usually critical and prefer to be kind and constructive – tough love is not usually your approach.

Famous people born on this day: Tupac Shakur, Phil Mickelson, Geronimo, Erich Segal, Ian Buchanan, Wally Joyner and Joyce Carol Oates.

1980 The Supreme Court declared that living organisms which are products of human ingenuity are patentable Diamond vs Chakrabaty

JUNE 17

Ruling planets are Mercury and Saturn.

Lucky colours are deep blue and black.

Lucky gems are blue sapphire, lapis lazuli and amethyst.

Intelligent, methodical, wise and measured you approach everything with a tenacity and you never quit. You are a keen learner and have good powers of insight. You enjoy communicating, reading and expanding your knowledge especially that to do with your field of expertise. You like to be prepared and armed with information. You have a wisdom beyond your years and this is reflected in a more serious side. You have wit and a keen sense of humour.

June 17 age very well and often work into their 70's as they love work and find it very rewarding. You concentrate well and are good at planning things in detail. You are a work-a-holic and often you just cannot switch off. You tend to demand a great deal from yourself and can be your own worst critic.

Those born on this day are often authorities in their field. You go after what you want with focus and determination and you overcome fears and a certain lack of self-belief by working extremely hard and refining your skills. Those on this day are not always gifted naturals, but you are people who rise to the top by virtue of hard work and the ability to hone talent.

June 17's grow in confidence with age and tend to enjoy life more as they get older. While you function very well socially you may actually prefer evenings in and may not seek out social events if not necessary. You like quality friendship rather than having a wide circle of friends just to prove how popular you are. You make a loyal and trustworthy friend.

Freeing yourself from your past is often your greatest challenge, you may have internalised a critical parent whose voice is always nagging in your head. Your challenge is to embrace who you are both accept and congratulate yourself for how far you have come. While your modesty is attractive you should never underestimate yourself. There are things in your life you need to make more of an effort to let go of so that you can enjoy your life more.

You are emotionally idealistic which can make it harder for you to understand those in your life, especially your family. Your early life may have not felt safe emotionally or may not have been emotionally supportive. You have a strong need to have your own family and will make many sacrifices to ensure your kids get a good start especially in terms of education.

You may often find it hard to find others who you totally relate to and this can mean you feel lonely, however your best relationships are those that grow over time and these are both strong and enduring. Stability and continuity are important to you, you are wise financially and have good business sense. Those on this day make good lawyers especially business lawyers. June 17 people are good with money and most often accumulate wealth and social standing.

There is a very spiritual side to this date of birth and also the promise that you can rise above all the difficulties of early life, with the ability to conquer any failure personally or professionally. There is also the promise of immortality in that your name may well live on after you.

Often June 17's struggle to show or talk about emotions and are often reserved. You take a while to be able to show affection and it is only with those you trust and connect with whom you can descend in to true passion with. June 17's are shy and often lonely, although you crave warm and affection. You often sacrifice true love for career and the pursuit of ambition. In family life a June 17 will make great sacrifices in order to provide and ensuring their children have a solid start in life is vital to you.

As partners, you are loyal and predictable and offer security and great friendship. Down to earth and with a great sense of humour, you are great to be around, however being a work-a-holic time with you can be at a premium.

To be seen as weak is something you will fight against all your life – you need to be seen as strong as a force to be reckoned with and will decry any actions which may give the impression of weakness or vulnerability.

Famous people born this day: Barry Manilow, Venus Williams, Lee Ryan, Newt Gingrich, Tory Burch, Igor Stavinsky, Joe Piscopo and Jason Patric.

1980 Atari's "Asteroids" and "Lunar Lander" are the first two video games to be copyright registered.

JUNE 18

Ruling planets are Mercury and Mars

Lucky colours are red, maroon and scarlet and autumn tones.

Lucky gems are red coral and garnet.

Direct and honest, you are a straight talker who calls it as you see it sometimes speaking without thinking first. You catch on fast and make quick deductions. You understand people from all walks of life. You are highly observant and sharp, not much gets beyond you. You are very good with words and can be a very effective and energetic speaker; you are good at quick fire debate and can think on your feet. While you are eloquent you are also warm and easy to get on with. You make friends fast and strike up a rapport with people easily.

You are impatient and can have flare ups of temper when things do not go as planned. You are very good at organising yourself and others and you are highly effective in management. You can be rather changeable and are prone to moodiness during which your behaviour is rather unpredictable. While some are confused by your contradictory nature, you are respected and people enjoy working with you. You have a powerfully positive vibe which inspires and motivates others and you get things done!

You rarely mince your words and what you see is what you get – this can seem a little abrasive for the more sensitive types and you may sometimes have to learn to be a little more diplomatic, however no one can ever be in any doubt of where they stand with you and your honesty should be appreciated.

You are not shy to go head to head in a heated debate and you will fight your corner. You are feisty and with your strong command of language and the facts you can be formidable. You are independent and will never allow others to dictate to you what you can think or do, you will rebel against any restrictions you see as unnecessary. While you can rebel, that does not mean you resent all authority as sometimes those on this day can be dedicated members of the military who enjoy the regimes – but the key is choice, if you chose a certain form of authority you will respect that, what you will never accept is anything forced on you.

You are strong willed and also practical and decisive in the way you operate. You dislike mental laziness and complacency in others and you have a strong work ethic. You love knowledge and also have no time for ignorance. You are a sympathetic person who will always find time to help someone you know. You crave the respect financial success brings and will strive to earn money...a lot of it. Even if born into wealth, you will want to prove you can make it on your own.

A woman born on this day will never be subservient or play second fiddle to anyone; she knows her own mind. Men and women on this day are natural leaders but need to learn to control their tempers and be more patient.

While your fiery nature and ability to think fast and make snap decisions usually serves you well; you may want to think about how sometimes holding back, staying silent and delaying a decision may be highly effective and take others by surprise – mix it up a little.

Those on June 18 are good with numbers and may well excel at maths and accounting; you are also good with your hands and can be highly skilled craftsmen; in addition you may work well with highly technical machinery.

You regard yourself as something of a trail blazer, setting trends and carving out new territory, you thrive on challenges and love to prove naysayers wrong. You are always striving for new methods and techniques of doing things that are faster and more effective. Passionate in love, you are also highly idealistic about love and will seek a partner who is affectionate, adventurous and who excites you.

Your life will be filled with changes and many new starts, but that is part of your nature and your destiny – you are always pushing forward and seeking, you don't have a reverse gear. You tend to leap before you look and that can create some problems but rarely any regrets and you bounce back.

You love speed and adventure – do take care as accidents while travelling or due to recklessness are possible for those on this day.

You must never allow materialism to destroy the spiritual side of your nature and you should also not be deaf to the call of sixth sense. June 18 are often so busy and so caught up in living yourr lives to the full, that you neglect your spiritual side.

There can be bitter differences and divides within your family and wider social unrest, war or economic collapse may have a great effect on your life. You may use 'divide and conquer' as a method of making your money or you may find that while others falter you actually thrive in times of social upheaval and revolution. There is a warning on this day of deception and betrayal by friends – so never trust anyone totally. June 18 may also be affected by natural events like floods, earthquakes, explosions and lightening. Your greatest asset in life must be learning to turn the other cheek; while fight nor flight is your default, you need to know when the best way is to let something go and walk away from it. While conflict may be a theme of your life; how you deal with it is a spiritual challenge. Be noble, be honest, be kind in the face of cruelty and you have fulfilled your destiny.

Remember the poem 'If' by Rudyard Kipling.

Famous People born on this day: Paul McCartney, Delia Smith, Roger Ebert, Isabella Rossellini, Carol Kane.

1935 ROLLS-ROYCE was trademark registered

JUNE 19

Ruling planet Mercury and the Sun.

Lucky colours are copper and gold.

Lucky gem is Ruby.

Unique, mischievous, playful and with a youthful spirit those on this day never grow old. You are filled with vitality and belief in yourself and you have ambition and determination. June 19 also have a vision and while it may be something vague at first life events will shape and define that vision. Physically strong and competitive this is also a great day for those with sporting ambitions.

Potential for you is huge, but committing yourself to one path in order to fulfil that potential can be hard. With multi talents and many different interests you may be pulled in so many different directions that you never actually commit long enough to one in order to see results. While your life is filled with promise and you have great ambitions for yourself, your ultimate successes may take longer to come your way than you have hoped and you must be patient.

You have an incredible memory. This is a day of the future and people born on this day embrace the changing world and are progressive in outlook, excited by change and highly adaptable.

Those on this day reject stereotypes and are usually a bit out there. You also reject dogma and question the value of tradition and religion. You are all about looking forward not back and believe better days lay ahead.

Women on this day are often feminists.

You are smart and have a sparkling personality which itself is a huge asset and which gets you noticed. You struggle to tie yourself down to one thing and distractions are a big problem for you. A very active social life can also be one of those distractions. You believe that one must have fun in life and live it to the full. You also believe in love and will make great sacrifices to keep a relationship going if you believe in it.

You are versatile and curious and enjoy learning new facts, new skills and meeting new people. June 19 enjoy being the centre of attention and often any attention will do; you can achieve more in life when your rally others to your side by being willing to share any glory you earn with them.

Criticism is not welcomed because is often deemed as a personal affront as June 19 are invested in what they are and proud of what they are, that pride is sometimes too easily wounded. Having respect is important to you and you enjoy organising and taking control of people and situations.

You have an individualistic flair and like to be noticed; you are a trendsetter who revels in holding original views or living a life style which is unusual or inspirational. You have a lot of front, but despite that bravado, you can be very vulnerable and tender hearted. You are a good problem solver and leader as little gets you down; you are skilled at finding solutions and are rarely defeatist.

You enjoy the limelight and make for a good performer – you may well have a shy side and yet externally you are gregarious and outgoing.

A strong day for political and military leadership due to the co-rulership of the Sun. June 19 will never be a conventional leader though; their style and approach will be unique and out of the box. Sometimes a little arrogant and bossy, you manage to get away with this due to your wit, humour and generosity. Try not to be heavy handed and pay more attention to working with others in a team. June 19 are not typically team players and their challenge is to learn how to bring everyone on board and work in a shared enterprise.

Success in life comes from knowing how to apply your knowledge constructively and also learning to share. Idle curiosity, irresponsibility and escapism pursuing personal follies can be your downfall.

June 19 is a day filled with fortune and promise and the overcoming of failure, sadness and disappointment is indicated.

Famous people born on this day: Paula Abdul, Boris Johnson, Lou Gehrig, Kathleen Turner, Rahul Ghandi, Blaise Pascal, Aung Sang Suu Kyi, Salman Rushdie, Wallis Simpson, Phylicia Rashad and Mia Sara.

1900 Michael Pupin is granted a patent for long distance telephony. 1940 "Brenda Starr," the first cartoon strip by a woman, appeared in a Chicago newspaper.

JUNE 20

Ruling planets are Mercury and Moon.

Lucky colours are cream and white and green.

Lucky gems are moonstone or pearl.

Kind, likable, responsible and warm, people are drawn to you and you are very emotionally intelligent. You can suss people out right away and decide what you make of them. You have strong feelings about things and these feelings can overwhelm your logic; you are a resolute person once you have made up your mind. You have great business acumen and are good with money, you are a good manager of resources and finances and a savvy investor. Your intuitive powers are well developed and you rely on gut feel. You socialise effectively but allow few into your inner social circle. You nurture friendships and are good at keeping in touch. You have a very caring side and are sensitive to the needs of others. You are highly adaptable, but often you bend yourself out of shape to keep others happy when you should stand up for yourself more and fight for your needs to be met.

You are a very changeable person and highly restless, you will seek a mate who can be a strong anchor for your fluctuating emotions. You are a resolute person who has a great deal of courage which is admirable – you can really dig deep when you have to. You have great self-belief and good timing and this can guarantee you success along with your ability to know people and understand their motivations. You are a keen worker who is diligent and reliable. You work well with others and enjoy work where you are emotionally involved.

Being in a love relationship is very important to you and will go to great lengths for the person you love. You are very family orientated and your relationship with your mother may colour all other relationships either in a good or bad way – it is very important for you to come to terms with any mother-issues you may be carrying around to ensure you excel in all other relationships.

You have a very active imagination and this is wonderful for writing and creativity in general however sometimes you can get so caught up in your imagination that it distorts your ability to deal with reality. You may also have strong escapist tendencies and a tendency to go into denial for long periods. You can sometimes over worry and imagine that the repercussions from your actions are much more severe than they are; you need to get the brakes on this habit you have of imagining the worst possible scenario. Often negative thinking is a defence for those on this day: a case of, if I expect the worst the reality has to be better. While this can work it can also cause you a great deal more stress than necessary.

Overanalysing both your own emotions and those of others can drain you and be counterproductive, learn to relax more and let things be. There is strong need for security within you and this can make you cautious and a little controlling however you are very responsible and well prepared.

You have excellent powers of observation and a great memory. You are also a wonderful storyteller and your understanding of emotion enables you to be a very good actor, performer, dancer or song-writer. Many on this day are psychic.

Not allowing yourself to be dragged down by the negativity of others or worry is your biggest challenge.

Your greatest successes are in the mental realm. Mental strength, astuteness and will power will help you to achieve success and financial security. You can be cunning and sometimes blinded by ego, but you are unstoppable.

You value loyalty extremely highly and do not forgive transgressors easily. Family ties and bonds as well as cultural heritage is important to you and you have a very traditional side. You are often a little suspicious and it takes a while to earn your trust. Your challenge in life is to deal with a deep seated insecurity and to develop more self-love and less fear of being judged. You enjoy work and if your early life had structure you are virtually assured of success.

Often with June 20 people there is a powerfully cathartic experience at some point in life which can alter your path and perspective quite dramatically – it is almost like an awakening or a call to action.

You may find that an experience you have awakens you to a calling you never knew you had and this can provide a powerful life direction. Delays and obstacles in your path should be dealt with with patience and should never get you down as they are ephemeral. Always have faith in yourself and your power to evolve and grow. You may have vivid precognitive dreams and you have the power to allow them to become reality or not though force of your will.

Financial security is more important to you than money and once that is achieved you will feel a certain freedom to fulfil yourself in non-material ways.

Famous people born this day: Nicole Kidman, Frank Lampard, Lionel Richie, Brian Wilson, Anne Murray, Errol Flynn, Chet Atkins and John Goodman.

1840 Samuel Morse was granted a patent for telegraphy signals.

THANK YOU SO MUCH FOR PURCHASING THIS BOOK. I HOPE I ENLIGHTENED AND ENTERTAINED YOU.

PLEASE LEAVE ME A REVIEW IF YOU HAVE TIME,

LOVE, LIGHT AND BEST WISHES, LISA LAZULI

Made in the USA
San Bernardino, CA
28 February 2018